A Short History of the Canadian North

Dr. Ed Whitcomb

From Sea to Sea Enterprises

Ottawa

Library and Archives Canada Cataloguing in Publication

Whitcomb, Edward A.
    A Short History of the Canadian North / Ed Whitcomb.

Includes bibliographical references and index.
ISBN 978-0-9865967-2-8

    1. Canada Northern—History. I. Title.

FC3956.W53 2011   971.9   C2011-903579-0

© From Sea To Sea Enterprises, 2010
2130 Dutton Crescent, Ottawa,
Ontario, Canada, K1J 6K4

Printed in Canada by Tina & Company, Ottawa

Table of Contents

This Book is Dedicated to the

people of the

Canadian North

Preface

This is the tenth in a series of history books on Canada's provinces and territories. The idea for this series first arose in 1969 when I moved to Nova Scotia. Being new to the province and knowing very little about it, I went looking for a short history book which would provide an outline of the development of my newly-adopted home. There was no such book. In fact, there were hardly any short histories of any of Canada's provinces. In 1975, I decided to write the sort of book I had been looking for, and began with my native province of Manitoba. Over 8,000 copies of that *Short History of Manitoba* have been sold, which suggests that I was not alone in wanting good, short provincial histories. The project to write histories of all the provinces was delayed by family and career, but the Centennials of Alberta and Saskatchewan put the series back on track, and the short histories of those provinces were published in 2005. It made sense to continue with western and then central Canada so *British Columbia* was published in 2006, *Ontario* in 2007, *Nova Scotia* in 2009, *New Brunswick* and *PEI* in 2010, and *The Canadian North* and *Newfoundland and Labrador* this year. The series will be completed when *Quebec* is published.

This *Short History of The Canadian North* is designed to provide the average reader with a quick but accurate survey of the broad outline of the region's development. The emphasis in this book is on the political and economic developments that shaped the territories as they are today, subjects such as the Aboriginals, exploration, the fur trade and whaling, the Klondike Gold Rush, the police and missionaries, the assertion of Canadian sovereignty, and economic stagnation in the early twentieth century. It explains the enormous impact of World War II, the attempts by the federal government to diversify and develop the economy, the slow development of self-rule and land claims, and the establishment of Nunavut complete the account.

Every historian has a point of view that determines which of the thousands of issues he or she will discuss, which of the millions of facts he or she will mention, and what things he or she will emphasize or ignore. This is essentially a political history, with some reference to economic and social developments, and it clearly emphasizes provincial rather than national or local issues. It is not "popular history," and does not include pictures. While the achievements of Northerners are documented, some criticisms are made of the heroes, politicians and groups who have shaped the province. In short, it is but one perspective on a very fascinating and complex society. My greatest hope is that this small book will encourage others to read more and to write more on the dozens of issues and perspectives necessary to obtain a full understanding of any society's development.

This account ends with the creation of Nunavut as a separate territory. Some readers will want it to cover more recent developments, but there is a point where history merges into political science or journalism. While we know the broad outline of recent events, we do not have access to Cabinet decisions, correspondence or the memoirs of most participants, and the secondary literature becomes less comprehensive. Many issues are still current, some still the subject of sharp debate, and many views on them are more subjective than objective. Much research has to be done and many books and articles written before the recent past falls into a proper historical perspective.

Many people helped with the preparation of this book. A number of professors, editors, analysts and experts read part or most of the text, and made many valuable corrections and suggestions. They include Dr. R. Matthew Bray, Dr. Kenneth Coates, Dr. Gerald Friesen, Jim McKillip, Dr. William Morrison, Margaret Poetschke, and Robert Poetschke. The cover design and map were prepared by Linda Turenne using a Natural Resources Canada map and the colours of the official flags of the three territories. Clifford Ford did the formatting and page layouts. Most helpful of all was my wife, Kai, whose support and patience makes these books possible. I alone am responsible for the weaknesses that remain in the book.

Ottawa, May, 2011.

Chapter 1

The Land and the People

The Canadian North is a geographic, administrative and political term. It is also an emotional expression in terms of Canadian nationalism and identity, "the True North Strong and Free" in the words of the national anthem. Though few Canadians actually visit the North, many view it as a distinctive and crucial part of themselves, see visits to the Canadian Shield as an annual ritual, have some "Vision of the North," and believe that asserting sovereignty over the North including its coastal water is a national imperative. In terms of geography, though, there is no agreement on any of the borders of the North. If it includes the Canadian Shield, then it extends south to the St Lawrence, the Great Lakes, and the western prairies. If it includes the land and water between the pie-shaped sector running from the Yukon-Alaska border to the North Pole and from the western tip of Greenland to the North Pole, then it is an enormous area indeed.

Politically and administratively, the Canadian North includes the lands north of the 60th parallel, which is the northern border of the four western provinces, plus the islands between that mainland and the North Pole. To the west, it borders on Alaska along the 141st meridian; to the east, it extends to Baffin Bay and Davis Strait which separate it from Greenland. There is disagreement as to whether Canada has sovereignty over the waterways between the islands, but the history that transpired in those waters is clearly part of the history of the Canadian North. Politically, the area has undergone a long evolution, with many adjustments to its borders. It now consists of three territories: the Yukon, covering 480,000 square kilometres, the Northwest Territories covering 1,140,000 square kilometres, and Nunavut covering 1,930,000 square kilometres. This is the history of that area and the people who lived and worked there.

The Canadian North covers over three and a half million square kilometres of land surface, 40% of the whole of Canada. The entire area is characterized by extreme cold and long winters, and, north of the Arctic Circle, periods of endless dark in winter and endless sunlight in summer. For a few months in summer, the surface soil warms enough to allow some vegetation to grow, but beneath that thin surface the soil is permanently frozen. That permafrost is like a rock barrier to the flow of water or the growth of tree roots. If it thaws, it often turns to mush, and is a major obstacle to the construction of infrastructure or buildings. The geography of the entire area can perhaps be understood best if it is divided into three regions: the Yukon, the Mackenzie River Valley, and the eastern Arctic and islands of the high Arctic, the latter also called the Canadian archipelago. Each of these regions can, of course, be sub-divided, and there are few distinct boundaries between them.

The Yukon is the most westerly part of Canada, the entire territory lying west of Victoria, British Columbia. There, the Rocky Mountains give way to a number of mountain ranges running roughly southeast to northwest. On the southwest, the St Elias Mountains separate the region from the Pacific Ocean, and some short rivers rise in the Yukon and flow into the Pacific. Mount Logan (6,000 metres), the highest mountain in Canada, is located there. Some of the mountain ranges are rich in minerals. On the east, the Mackenzie Mountains separate the Yukon from the Mackenzie River Valley, with some rivers such as the Liard flowing eastward into the Mackenzie River. The region is dominated by the Yukon plateau and the Yukon River, which rises in British Columbia, flows northwest across the Yukon, then through Alaska to the Bering Sea. It is 3,200 kilometres long, over 2,800 of that navigable to the rapids above Whitehorse, 800 kilometres of it in the Yukon. A number of major tributaries such as the Pelly and Porcupine provide transportation routes through the mountains, and are partly navigable. To the north, the land slopes down to the Beaufort Sea. The climate suffers from extreme cold in winter, but is warmed by winds from the Pacific. Rainfall is not abundant, but almost half the territory is forested, and the region is relatively rich in wildlife.

The Mackenzie River Valley drains an enormous area including central eastern British Columbia and northern Alberta via the Peace River, and northern Alberta and Saskatchewan via the Athabasca River. It contains two of the largest lakes in Canada: Great Slave and Great Bear. The Mackenzie River, which flows out of Great Slave Lake, is the longest river in Canada (1,700 kilometres), but the distance from its mouth to its origins in the headwaters of the Peace River is 4,200 kilometres. The Delta where it touches the Beaufort Sea is over 200 kilometres long, the largest river delta in the country. The river basin was scraped by glaciers, leaving little soil and numerous lakes, bogs, and twisted rivers full of rapids. The climate is milder than that of the eastern Arctic, and much of the region is therefore below the tree line. The territory contains important mineral resources and extensive oil and gas reserves, but economic development has always been restricted by remoteness, high costs, and problems with transportation and construction.

Several hundred kilometres east of the Mackenzie region, the land surface starts to feature tundra, scrub brush, wind-swept rocks, muskeg, numerous lakes and swamps, and a jumble of streams and rivers that flow north to the Arctic Sea or east to Hudson Bay. The southwest corner of it lies below the tree line which runs diagonally from east southeast to west northwest. Towards

Hudson Bay a sub-region known as The Barrens covers land so scarred it supports little wildlife. Generally, the farther north one travels, the more barren the land becomes. Baffin Island dominates the eastern end of this region, and is the largest island in Canada. Its coast is characterized by inlets, the largest being Frobisher Bay and Cumberland Sound. Victoria and Banks Islands dominate the western end of this region.

To the north of these islands lies Lancaster Sound, and to the north of it lie the major islands of Ellesmere, Devon, Melville and Prince Patrick. This region is subject to extremes of cold and wind. The sea is frozen for over 10 months of the year, and often jammed with pack ice during summer. The sea, however, contains rich food resources—an abundant supply of shrimp that feed off plankton and provide food for whales, seals, and walruses which, in turn, are the food source for polar bears. The frozen sea also provides for relatively easy transportation between islands and with the mainland. The land mass produces little vegetation other than lichens and mosses, the food supply of caribou and musk-ox.

The Canadian North was discovered, explored, settled, and developed by people who came from Asia. Its first inhabitants were First Nations who crossed from Siberia to Alaska when low seas exposed a land bridge across the present Bering Strait. There is no agreement on when or how these first migrations occurred. It may have been as much as 30,000 years ago, but glaciers confined those first North Americans to Alaska and the Yukon until 11-12.000 years ago. Then, they began to migrate south probably along the eastern edge of the Rocky Mountains and east into the North American prairies and up into the woodlands. These Dene people spoke Athapaskan, but separate dialects developed which distinguished different groups. They included the Tagish, Tutchone, Tlingit, and Kutchin in the Yukon, and the Slave, Cree, Chipewyan, and Copper farther east. These Aboriginal peoples gathered in large groups in spring and summer to fish on rivers and lakes or to hunt sea mammals such as seals and walruses. In winter they went inland in smaller groups to hunt caribou and moose, a diet supplemented with smaller animals, birds, and berries.

Survival depended on communal living in families, extended families or larger groups. Harmony was essential for survival, and First Nations society emphasized cooperation, sharing, equality, friendship, and behaviour that reinforced the community. There was a clear division of labour, but women occupied important roles and were not necessarily subordinate. Children were raised in the extended family, and learned by such forms of discipline as scolding, and peer-pressure. Elders were respected. Decision-making was largely by consensus, with the views of elders probably carrying more weight. Leaders were selected for specific tasks such as hunting or warfare, and religious leaders known as shamans fulfilled an extremely important role in terms of spiritual, psychological, and physical health.

The First Nations saw their environment as a unity of which they were part. They had well developed views of their origin, life after death, and the role of spirits in their lives. Everything had a spirit which had to be respected. Animals were killed out of necessity, never for sport, and their spirits were honoured. Every part of the animal was used—hide for clothes, sinew for thread, bones and antlers for tools, and bladders for carrying water. Caribou hides made far more suitable clothing for the North than the clothing worn by Europeans. Climate limited the availability of wildlife, which meant that the First Nations were nomadic except in a few areas rich in wildlife such as the Mackenzie Delta. That nomadic life sharply reduced the capacity to accumulate goods other than tents, clothes, tools and weapons.

The Inuit were different from First Nations physically, culturally, and linguistically. They probably came from Siberia to Alaska by boat, and gradually spread along the Arctic coast to Greenland, remaining primarily sea-based people though they hunted caribou far into the interior. With the sea frozen for most of the year, they ranged widely over land, water, and ice in search of food. Archaeologists have identified three waves of Inuit, each one absorbing or melding into the previous group. The first group which had mastered the art of survival in the extreme cold arrived in the western Arctic over 4,000 years ago and have been named Paleo-Eskimos. The second wave arrived around 3,000 years ago. They have been named Dorset Eskimos after archaeological digs at Cape Dorset, people who lived in igloos or huts made of turf, used kayaks, and burnt whale oil in soapstone vessels for heat, light and cooking.

The last group known as the Thule arrived around 1,000 years ago, also from Siberia, and are the direct ancestors of the Inuit. They brought with them sealskin kayaks, larger open boats known as umiaks, and sleds pulled by dog teams. They hunted whales with harpoons attached to floats made from animal bladders, which tired the whales to the point that they could be killed. They used bows and arrows and hunted seals, walruses, caribou, musk-ox, and smaller animals, and they caught a variety of fish. In winter the Inuit made igloos of snow with windows of ice; in summer they lived in tents made out of caribou hide and whalebone.

The Thule were more technologically sophisticated than previous migrants, having mastered the art of making waterproof boots, double-layer skin clothes that could withstand Arctic temperatures, sun glasses, and copper knives. Like the First Nations, they killed only what they had to, saw themselves as part of an environment every part of which required respect, and were deeply religious. Over the centuries, non-Aboriginals found them very friendly and easy to work and live with, but very fierce if they perceived an outsider to be a threat. Their ancient culture survived well into the twentieth century because of isolation, because the culture suited the environment, and because they were flexible in adapting elements of European technology and lifestyle into that culture.

The Canadian North was explored by the First Nations and Inuit from west to east, and from below the tree line northward into the tundra and then into the Arctic islands. These people knew the river and lake systems and portages, the islands and the waterways between them. They ranged over vast areas, and traded food, tools, clothes, and weapons with neighbouring groups. They had clear ideas of the value of different products, and began trading with Europeans as soon as the latter appeared. They had no written records of the landscape, but a thorough knowledge of it was part of their cultural heritage.

Chapter 2

Exploration

The first European to discover the North was probably the Norseman, Leif Ericson, around 1000 AD. The Vikings were suffering from over-population and had expanded westward to Iceland and Greenland. Ericson explored farther west, touching on Baffin Island and Labrador. There were other explorations, but they did not lead to permanent settlement or annual visits to fish or explore, and the knowledge of North America seems to have disappeared in Europe. Following John Cabot's re-discovery of Newfoundland in 1497, European fishermen came in large numbers to the Atlantic coast of North America. Cabot's goal was to find a route to the riches of the Orient. Since the east coast of North America blocked that route, great effort went into finding a way around it, namely, a Northwest Passage.

Fishermen probed the Labrador coast, but the first European to seek a route around North America was Sir Martin Frobisher, a privateer, pirate, fortune-hunter, and con artist. He arrived in 1576 hoping to find valuable minerals, a route to Asia, and possibly Aboriginals eager to trade. He discovered Baffin Island and the Bay which bears his name. He met Inuit who traded readily with the strangers. He kidnapped one Inuk and took him back to England where he soon died. Frobisher took rock samples back to England. Competent assayers said that the rocks were worthless, but one was found who said they might contain gold. That led to another expedition in 1577, some further exploration, the first mining operation in North America north of Mexico, and a larger sample of rocks to take back. Some assayers in London said the rock might contain gold, leading to a third voyage in 1578. Even more worthless rock was taken back to tarnish Frobisher's reputation, but his major achievements were sailing some 200 kilometres into Hudson Strait and being the first to see Baffin Island which gave the English Crown a claim to it.

In 1585, 1586, and 1587 John Davis attempted to find the Northwest Passage, exploring the strait that bears his name, and sailing as far north as the 72nd parallel. Twenty years later, Thomas Baffin sailed another 500 kilometres north before his progress was blocked by ice. In 1607, Henry Hudson sailed through the strait that bears his name. He entered a giant body of water, since named after him, but found no exit on the western side leading to Asia. Hudson's crew mutinied and set him adrift, never to be seen again. In 1670, King Charles II gave the newly-formed Hudson's Bay Company (HBC) a monopoly on the trade of the entire region whose waters drained into Hudson

Bay. Aboriginal peoples were willing to come to the few posts that the company established on the coast, so the HBC wasted no money exploring the hinterland. Over the decades that complacent attitude raised some concern, but the company avoided action until French fur traders based in Montreal began to enter the Arctic watershed northwest of the Great Lakes, threatening to outflank the company. In 1722, the HBC sent a ship to explore the northwest coast of Hudson Bay. It failed to find a passage leading westward, and came to grief on Southampton Island where the entire crew perished. Another expedition found no viable route west of Southampton Island, and a disappointed captain named the harbour Repulse Bay.

Rumours of copper deposits and a great sea prompted the HBC to try an overland exploration, to be headed by a young officer named Samuel Hearne. His first attempt in November, 1769, failed when his guides deserted him. A second trip a year later took him far to the west into the Barrens where he was robbed. A Chipewyan chief—Matonabbee—saved him from almost certain starvation. Matonabbee was planning a trip northwest of Fort Prince of Wales (Churchill), so Hearne joined him. While European explorers tried to reach their destinations by the shortest route, First Nations planned their trips according to the availability of wildlife no matter how much that added to the distance. The Chipewyan party with Hearne in it therefore advanced west to the Barrens and then down the Coppermine River. They did not find deposits of copper, but did encounter an Inuit camp. The First Nations and Inuit were enemies, and all the Inuit were massacred. They then moved west and north, Hearne becoming the first European to see the Arctic shore. They went farther west, where he became the first explorer to see Great Slave Lake. The incredible journey took 32 months and covered some 6,000 kilometres. Hearne claimed the lands for the HBC, perhaps doubling the area of its original charter.

After Britain's conquest of New France in 1763, British merchants joined hands with French Canadian fur traders in Montreal to create new companies. The most successful of them, the North West Company or NWC, expanded up the Saskatchewan River. In 1778, First Nations showed one of its agents, Peter Pond, the Methye Portage between the Saskatchewan and Athabascan River basins. The First Nations talked of a great river that flowed westward out of a great lake, and Alexander Mackenzie was tasked with exploring it. On 3 June 1789, he left Fort Chipewyan on Lake Athabasca, travelled down to Great Slave Lake, and followed the great river westward. Unfortunately, it turned north, but Mackenzie followed it to its mouth on the Beaufort Sea. He is alleged to have named it the River of Disappointment, but it soon bore his name. The trip had taken over 100 days and covered 5,000 kilometres. Four years later First Nations led Mackenzie over their trade routes to the Pacific, making him the first white man to cross North America north of Mexico.

West of the Mackenzie River Valley, the Russians had an active fur trade which tapped the interior from the Alaskan coast. The HBC decided to challenge them, but first it had to explore the region. In 1840, Robert Campbell travelled from the Mackenzie River up the Liard, which was quite unsuitable for transportation, over the watershed, and down the Pelly River to its confluence with a river the local people called the Youcon. Five years later, John Bell travelled west from the Mackenzie Delta and down the Porcupine River to the Yukon River. In 1845, the HBC sent John Rae to make an intensive investigation of the Arctic watershed. He travelled some 35,000 kilometres over four years, criss-crossing the territory from the Mackenzie River to Hudson Bay. The success of these explorers was based on the fact that they lived and traveled like the Aboriginals, and took their advice. Over the next half century, fur traders, trappers, missionaries, and prospectors added much information about the North and corrected and filled in gaps on maps.

Earlier attempts to find the Northwest Passage failed, but they also demonstrated that even if such a route were found, it would not provide a viable shipping route to the Pacific because of the ice. In the early nineteenth century, however, the search resumed as a matter of national pride and scientific curiosity. Britain, for example, offered a reward, which produced a number of expeditions, more accurate mapping of the islands and waterways, and considerable loss of life. These voyages seemed to confirm that there was a passage, but not its location. In 1845, the Royal Navy selected John Franklin to lead a major expedition. He was given the job in spite of considerable evidence of his incompetence and previous failures. He clung to the British practice of sending well-equipped ships and using them as bases, rather than the practice of using dog sleds to follow established Aboriginal routes while living off the land.

Franklin's first two voyages—in 1818 and 1819—added to knowledge about the coastline east of the Coppermine River and west of the Mackenzie River. In 1845, he brought a large expedition with enough canned European food to last three years so they would not have to live off the land. That may have been a fatal mistake, because the ship became jammed in the ice off King William Island and the crew had to abandon it. All of them died, some having prolonged their lives by resorting to cannibalism. The search for Franklin became one of the greatest manhunts in Canadian history, with some thirty expeditions over a period of a century. It was only in the 1980s that the remains of several of the crew were found, a discovery that confirmed the rumour of cannibalism. Like Hudson and many other explorers, Franklin's body was never found.

In the 1880s, the Canadian Senate launched a massive investigation of the mainland from Alaska to Hudson Bay. The Geological Survey of Canada did extensive work and was served by a number of excellent scientists such as George Dawson. It made the resources of the North well known throughout Canada. Joseph Tyrrell and his brother James studied the rivers, lakes, people, and resources of the Barrens. In 1887, William Ogilvie staked the border with Alaska and then surveyed and mapped the Yukon River basin and the Liard River. In 1907, the Senate launched another study of the North.

In the late nineteenth century, exploration in the high Arctic accelerated, driven by the search for the Passage, the quest to be the first to reach the North Pole, a desire to claim or defend sovereignty over the islands, the possibility that exploitable mineral resources might be found, and perhaps above all, personal ambition. In 1875-76, a British expedition explored Ellesmere Island. Between 1878 and 1880, an American team travelled from Marble Island to Repulse Bay and King William Island by dog sled. Retired American Naval officer Robert Peary explored northern Baffin Island and reached the North Pole in 1909. More importantly, the Norwegian Roald Amundsen finally sailed through one of the branches of the Northwest Passage in 1903-05. He brought back much valuable information, including the final proof that it could not be used for navigation.

Between 1898 and 1902, another Norwegian—Otto Sverdrup—explored and mapped 2,800 kilometres of the coast of Ellesmere Island and other islands in the high Arctic. He claimed them for Sweden, which then controlled Norway, posing a serious challenge to Canada's claim to sovereignty. This finally prompted Ottawa to invest some money and effort in Arctic exploration. In 1903, the Geological Survey examined Cumberland Sound, Foxe Basin, Baffin Bay, Ellesmere Island, Lancaster Sound, and Somerset Island. In 1904, the Canadian navigator Joseph Bernier began the first of four expeditions to Lancaster Sound, Pond Inlet, Melville Island, McClure Strait, and Prince of Wales Strait.

The next major expedition was undertaken by Vilhjalmur Stefansson, who was deeply interested in asserting Canadian authority, rolling back the fog of ignorance about the North, discovering islands, developing the economy, propagating his view that the Arctic was actually quite a hospitable place, and above all, covering himself with glory. He had made successful trips in 1906 and 1908, especially to Victoria Island. He had also developed a reputation as a great public speaker or, in the eyes of his many critics, a shameless propagandist. His approach to the Canadian government to fund an expedition coincided with Ottawa's determination to take a more active role in the region, and the Canadian Arctic Expedition was born.

This expedition, which lasted from 1913 to 1918, faced serious problems from the start. Stefansson wanted to concentrate on geography and the islands while the government and the experts wanted to concentrate on scientific knowledge and the mainland. The solution was to split the expedition in two, with Stefansson exploring islands and a second team under R.M. Anderson exploring the mainland. Three ships were sent to Herschel Island, one for Stefansson's expedition and two for Anderson's. While Stefansson was off hunting, his ship became entrapped in ice, was carried across the Arctic to Siberia, and sank with a loss of 16 of the 28 men. Stefansson then sought supplies from the other two ships, further annoying Anderson and his experts. They did, however, provide him with supplies, and he left with a dog team and one associate.

Stefansson went north over the ice for 300 kilometres, then turned east, discovering some islands which he claimed for Canada. His journeys took him to numerous islands: Banks, Borden, Brock, Herschel, Lougheed, Mackenzie King, Meighen, Melville, Prince Patrick, and Victoria. He accumulated an impressive amount of information on the region, its people, and resources. He later annoyed experts, police, and missionaries by publishing a book called *The Friendly Arctic* which suggested, quite incorrectly, that the region was less dangerous than it was. He assumed that because he could live off the land, large numbers of people could, ignoring the fact that the wildlife could only support a small number of people and they had to be experts to survive. Nevertheless, he achieved his primary goal of gaining fame, and exploited that reputation by spending the rest of his life on speaking tours. At the same time, Anderson's expedition criss-crossed the mainland, filling in gaps on maps and collecting an enormous amount of information. By 1920, the task of exploring the Canadian North had been largely completed. It had taken three and a half centuries and enormous expenditure and loss of life, but it left Canadian history enriched with the names of some of the world's greatest explorers.

Chapter 3

The Fur Trade and Whaling

The fur trade began in the Canadian North as a supplement to fishing and whaling. When Frobisher first arrived, Inuit came to the European ships and offered fish, meat, furs, walrus ivory, and other products for whatever the whalers wished to give up. Whalers quickly learned what the Inuit wanted, brought those products on subsequent trips, and carried on trade as a sideline to whaling. Fur pelts were a very valuable product in Europe because of a high demand for hats made of the felt from the pelts, and the fur trade proved to be immensely profitable.

These high profits have led some people to assume that the Aboriginals were unfairly exploited. In fact, the substitution of a musket for a bow and arrow represented a phenomenal improvement in technology, as did the acquisition of steel knives, hatchets, needles, pots and pans, and thread to replace sinew. The trade was extremely beneficial and profitable for both parties. The Inuit were excellent traders. If they concluded that an object was worth a certain number of furs, the deal was made, and if they felt the Europeans were asking too much, they walked away. Whalers and fishermen could also walk away from a negotiation, but Europeans who came specifically to trade had no choice but to provide what the Aboriginals wanted at a price acceptable to them.

The high profits made by the fishermen and whalers caught the attention of entrepreneurs in London. A group of them organized a company and obtained the support of one of the most powerful figures at court, Prince Rupert, the cousin of King Charles II. With good connections in business and at court, and sound financial support, that company obtained in 1670 a monopoly from the King for the fur trade over all rivers draining into Hudson Bay. The firm was the Hudson's Bay Company or HBC, and the region was named Rupert's Land. It covered roughly one quarter of North America, from northeast Quebec to the Rockies and into the prairies of the present United States.

Since First Nations were eager to trade furs for European goods, the HBC built a few posts at the mouths of large rivers and let the First Nations come to them to trade. The Cree lived near Hudson Bay, and thus became the first partners of the company. The Cree in turn traded HBC goods with the First Nations farther inland, and people in the whole area drained by those rivers was soon exporting furs to London in exchange for HBC goods. The Cree did not want other groups to trade directly with the company, and were sufficiently powerful and numerous to maintain their role as middlemen for over a century.

The HBC was eventually forced to alter its strategy when French fur traders based in Montreal began to compete along the watershed between Hudson Bay and the St. Lawrence-Great Lakes basin. The HBC had to send traders into the interior and establish more posts. The competition became intense after Britain conquered New France and new companies arose combining English finances, markets, and trade goods with French Canadian trade routes and close relations with the First Nations. In the 1780s, the North West Company (NWC) emerged as the dominant Montreal-based fur trading giant. It expanded up the Saskatchewan River and into the Lake Athabasca region which drained into the Arctic watershed. Fort Chipewyan on Lake Athabasca became the base for a string of trading posts including Fort Good Hope, the first post on the lower Mackenzie River.

The HBC had to match the NWC, and the Aboriginals played the two companies off against each other. Both companies had to offer better firearms and other products including liquor, and extend easier credit. Competition became violent, with traders from one company ambushing canoe brigades from the other. Costs mounted, the price of furs increased, and profits were driven down. The HBC sent its trade goods up the Nelson River to Lake Winnipeg, and then up the Saskatchewan to the Mackenzie River Valley; the NWC sent its goods up the Ottawa River, across the Great Lakes, over Red River and up the Saskatchewan. It took seven years to send goods from the warehouses in London to the posts in northern Canada and ship the furs back to London.

While the NWC demonstrated initiative, speed, and imagination, the HBC had shorter lines of communication and a stronger financial base. The competition stretched both companies to the breaking point, and in 1821, the two companies amalgamated under the name Hudson's Bay Company. It then combined the two operations, eliminated the Montreal route and the duplicate posts, dismissed surplus traders, raised prices, and stopped supplying liquor. This rationalization was executed by the ruthlessly efficient Governor of the Northern District—George Simpson—who effectively governed a large part of the Canadian North for four decades.

The fur trade soon settled down to a routine. Traders managed their posts, traded with the local people, sent the annual shipment of furs down to York Factory, supplied anyone else who visited, and kept accurate records. Fur traders often formed relationships with local woman, and the growing number of offspring became the basis for the Métis nation. At first the fur trade did not radically transform Aboriginal society as people carried on their traditional lifestyles, only with better equipment. Gradually, however, they became more dependent on European goods including food and clothing.

The HBC expanded down the Mackenzie River Valley and into the tributaries that came from the west such as the Liard River. Local people talked of a vast territory west of the Mackenzie Mountains, where rich fur supplies were being tapped by Russian companies on the Pacific coast of Alaska. In 1825, diplomats established the border between Alaska and British territories as a line beginning at the 60th parallel and running north on the 141st meridian. In the 1830s, the HBC began sending officers in search of the great river that flowed westward through this region. Robert Campbell opened Fort Selkirk where the Pelly River joins the Yukon, and in 1847, Alexander Murray Bell established Fort Youcon at the mouth of the Porcupine River.

Fort Youcon was actually well inside Alaska, but the Russians did not have the resources to challenge the HBC in eastern Alaska. The Aboriginals near the HBC posts became middlemen for those more distant. They opposed the building of more HBC posts, and did not cooperate with HBC explorers in order to keep trade routes secret. They repeatedly told the HBC that the Russians were closer and more active than they actually were, creating the impression that the HBC's position was very tenuous. To the southwest, the Tlingit dominated the fur trade between posts on the Pacific coast and the Aboriginals in the interior. The HBC could not break Tlingit control of the passes, and furs from that part of the Yukon continued to flow westward to the Pacific. To enforce their position, the Tlingit destroyed Fort Selkirk, a rare occurrence but a warning that had to be heeded. In 1867, the United States purchased Alaska from Russia, and Americans soon set out to exploit its resources. The HBC had to abandon Fort Youcon and move upstream. The Americans were excellent and aggressive traders, and had the advantage of controlling the Yukon River. The HBC found that it could not compete, and American fur traders gained control of most of the Yukon region.

The fur trade gradually opened up the North as the network of HBC posts spread from Hudson Bay across the prairies, down the Mackenzie River Valley, and then west into the Yukon and east and north into the central Arctic. Fur trading and trapping were usually life-long occupations, and the posts led to the first white settlements in the North. Aboriginals camped beside the posts when they came to trade, and some of them became part-time labourers supplying the posts with food and wood and acting as guides. The fur trade rested on an elaborate transportation system. Naturally, it carried news, becoming the North's communications system. Portages around rapids evolved into wagon trails and eventually into roads. Bigger boats gradually replaced canoe brigades, and by the 1880s, the HBC was using steam-driven paddle boats on the major rivers. The traders became a major source of information for government and police when the latter institutions developed. When starvation threatened

Aboriginal bands, governments distributed rations through the HBC, making their agents quasi civil servants.

The British government transferred Rupert's Land to the new Canadian government in 1869 along with the Arctic islands a decade later. These momentous political changes had little effect on the fur trade, which remained under the firm control of the HBC. It was, however, earning such profits that other companies began entering the field in the late nineteenth century, a major one being the French company of Revillon Frères. Competition led to higher incomes for the Aboriginals followed by over-hunting and a serious depression in the industry in the 1890s. Changes in fashion made old staples such as beaver pelts less valuable, but demand arose for fox, mink, and martin, changes that made the fur trade in the far North relatively more profitable.

The HBC continued to evolve as it always had, slowly, carefully, and successfully. Competition led to a change in the fur trade, with less trading of furs for goods and more purchases for cash. This created more flexibility on both sides, and HBC posts became retail stores which also purchased pelts rather than fur trading posts which sometimes sold goods. As Aboriginals became more dependent on European goods and more aware of them, they demanded a greater variety. That trend was reinforced by the growing presence of non-Aboriginals in the North: trappers, traders, explorers, missionaries, tourists, and government officials, all of whom shopped at the HBC store.

High prices and easier access attracted more and more non-Aboriginal trappers. They often took a short-term view, over-trapping an area and moving on, and using poison, a practice which horrified the Aboriginals. The federal government enacted regulations to control trapping and banned the use of poison. It was difficult to enforce such rules, however, and the wildlife continued to decline. By the late 1880s, many Aboriginals were facing starvation. The selling of meat was banned, and hunters and trappers had to obtain licences.

In the early twentieth century the continued demand for furs and the depletion of wildlife in traditional areas led the HBC to expand systematically into the Arctic islands. Throughout this area it was the dominant company in fur trading, retailing, transportation, and communications. In the 1920s, another change in fashion made the white fox an extremely desirable commodity, and its home was the far North. During this period, good trappers were earning more than industrial workers in the factories of Ontario and Quebec. That brief period of prosperity ended with the Great Depression. The price of furs dropped dramatically, independent traders went bankrupt, and once again many Aboriginals faced starvation. The HBC weathered the storm in part because it had diversified its operations, but the fur trade gradually lost its status as the dominant economic function in the Canadian North. It continued as an important element in the northern economy, only to be further damaged in the second half of the twentieth century by the animal rights movement.

Whaling began at the same time as the fur trade. Whale oil was in great demand in Europe and North America for lighting and as a lubricant. Lady's corsets were in fashion, and they required a plastic-like substance made from the Bowhead whale's baleen or cartilage. Whaling began along the coast of Labrador and gradually expanded north and west to Davis Strait and the coast of Baffin Island. In the eastern Arctic it peaked in the 1830s and 1840s, but the introduction of steam power after the 1850s allowed whaling to expand into the high Arctic.

Whaling was a very dangerous occupation. Large ships faced all the risks of navigation in the northwest Atlantic: storms, high winds, icebergs, and inadequate charting and maps. Ships risked being caught in pack ice or frozen in for the long winter, a situation that could crush a ship. The whales were hunted by harpoon from small row boats, an extremely hazardous occupation immortalized in the book *Moby Dick*. Blubber was cut from the whales and boiled on ship or on shore to extract the oil. The Inuit welcomed the whalers, and took jobs on the ships and whaling boats, supplied the whalers with food, and acted as guides. They also scavenged things left on shore by the whalers, their attitude being that if no one was using an object, then it had been abandoned and anyone could take it. Europeans often regarded this as theft, a conflict of cultural views that endured.

The whaling industry then shifted to the Pacific, and American whalers pushed farther and farther north towards the northern shores of Alaska. Moving eastward along that coast proved extremely dangerous. In the 1880s, whalers discovered that there was a good winter harbour at Pauline Cove on Herschel Island, off the coast of the Yukon. Ships could travel from American Pacific ports in the late spring, harvest whales in the summer, spend the winter at Pauline Cove, harvest for a second summer, and sail back around Alaska before freeze-up. The Beaufort Sea contained enormous stocks of whales, and in 1891 the first ships to make the trip sold their cargoes at enormous profits. Over a dozen ships were soon wintering at Pauline Cove.

Trade began immediately with the Inuit, with the exchange of American goods for caribou meat and furs. With over 500 men spending the winter, the demand for food was great, and the Inuit were soon hunting caribou as much as 300 kilometres inland. Unlike the HBC, the whalers viewed the fur trade as a short-term opportunity to add greater profit to their voyages. They traded repeating rifles and alcohol, and their high demand for meat and furs soon depleted the region to the disadvantage of the Inuit who still lived off the land.

Relations soon developed between the whalers and Inuit women. Ship's captains took mistresses, a position regarded by the women as carrying prestige, but the crews were forbidden to have relationships. Captains could not, however, prevent crews from socializing with the Inuit, and alcohol flowed freely as people escaped the boredom of the endless winter nights. Inuit men did not seem to object to these relationships, and the violence that did accompany the socializing was between members of the crew rather than between crews and Inuit.

Missionaries believed that sex was only acceptable within marriage, and therefore condemned the relationships and activities on Herschel Island. They demanded that the federal government send police to put an end to the alleged debauchery and abuse. Ottawa ignored their demands, and when police were stationed at Pauline Cove, they concluded that the missionaries were exaggerating. It was difficult to believe that the local people were being abused when they welcomed the arrival of new ships every spring.

Royal North West Mounted Police (RNWMP) were sent to Herschel island in 1904 not because of problems with the Inuit, alcohol, or violence, but because the presence of up to 1,000 American whalers posed a potential threat to Canadian sovereignty. In 1903, Canada lost a bitter dispute over the Alaska Panhandle boundary, and had no intention of giving Americans any new grounds to claim Canadian territory. The RNWMP were sent to Fort McPherson and Herschel Island to show the flag, enforce Canadian laws, and collect customs because paying customs demonstrated that the ships accepted Canadian sovereignty. Captains were asked to identify goods they had brought in for trade, and were levied a nominal duty on those goods.

The police also found the captains helpful with enforcing laws. Captains welcomed Canadian police and provided quarters for them. Whaling crews were often recruited in the rough taverns along the waterfronts of American ports. Fighting, drunkenness, alcohol abuse, mutiny, and desertion were common threats to the whaling industry, and the captains were happy to see Canadian police bring some degree of order. The police were successful because, paradoxically, their lack of power, numbers, and equipment left them no option but to take a realistic and flexible approach to the enforcement of federal laws, many of which made little sense in the North. They concentrated on the two things that mattered: asserting sovereignty and dealing with violent crime. They made no attempt to enforce Canada's stringent prohibition laws, and they ignored the missionaries' complaints about immorality. Some police had intimate relations with Inuit women, suggesting that their views about sex were closer to those of the whalers than to those of the missionaries.

As in other areas, the ships harvested as many whales as possible, quickly depleting stocks, and moving farther east and north. By the early twentieth century, the industry was in decline in the Beaufort Sea. Fortunately for the remaining stocks of whales, by that time petroleum products were replacing whale oil for lubricating and lighting, and corsets were not quite as fashionable. By 1910, whaling was no longer a major industry in the Canadian North, and the Inuit turned to the fur trade to maintain the flow of European goods to which they were becoming accustomed. The whalers, however, had also brought diseases, and the Inuit they first met on Herschel Island were decimated. The whalers replaced them with Inuit from Alaska. Overhunting to supply the whalers seriously depleted the wildlife on which the Inuit depended, and when the whalers left, many faced starvation. The whole whaling episode reflected an unfortunate pattern, with outsiders descending in large numbers on the North to exploit a resource, spending their wages and profits in the south, seriously disrupting Inuit life and culture, and leaving little of value when the resource was depleted. But it was not until 1972 that the federal government banned non-Aboriginals from whaling in the North.

Chapter 4

The Klondike Gold Rush

The Klondike Gold Rush of 1898 was one of the few purely Canadian developments that attracted world-wide attention. It had all the ingredients of great drama: fabulous riches, enormous challenges, winding creeks, rushing rivers, spectacular mountains, lawlessness, saloons, dance halls, prostitutes, gamblers, con-artists, and the North-West Mounted Police. When news of the strike reached the south, thousands of people lined up on the docks to catch a ride on any boat heading for Alaska. Miners, adventurers, and dreamers headed for Canada from Europe and Australia. Mythology intertwined with reality, reinforced by the wonderful poetry of Robert Service. The legend survived, and the lure of the North became the basis of the Yukon's greatest industry—tourism.

After the California gold rush of 1848, miners concluded that more gold would be found in the coastal mountains running north all the way to Alaska. Discoveries in northern California and then on the Fraser River confirmed their view. Prospectors were looking for placer gold, nuggets and flakes that had washed down from some mother lode in a mountain. Placer gold settled into the sand, gravel, and muck of the creek and river beds and banks. It could be found simply by putting some of that material in a pan and swishing it around in water. As the dirty water spilled over the sides, it took the lighter sand and soil with it, leaving the heavier gold at the bottom. In 1872, miners began entering the Yukon. Some were rewarded, and more came, convinced that a major gold field was nearby. By 1882, fifty miners were working the Yukon, and by the mid-1890s, over 1,000 were there.

They concentrated in a community called Forty Mile, where the Fortymile River joins the Yukon River, on the Alaskan side of the border. Forty Mile was not a lawless, frontier town. Mining was a hard profession, and people took it up because they hoped to get rich and because they enjoyed the lifestyle, the freedom, and the outdoors. Their survival depended on personal security, and they had unwritten laws protecting claims and possessions, and rules that anyone in need had to be helped, that food had to be left in cabins and camps, that doors had to be left unlocked, and that news of a strike had to be shared.

The vast majority of miners were American, and as the number of miners increased, Canadians in the region and in the federal government became concerned with the threat they posed to Canadian sovereignty. Canada was involved in a dispute with the United States over the Alaskan Panhandle, thousands of American whalers were operating in the Beaufort Sea, and those who could remember the Alamo knew that the United States had used illegal immigrants to wrest Texas from Mexico. In 1894, Ottawa sent two members of the NWMP—Inspector Charles Constantine and Staff Sergeant Charles Brown—to assert Canadian authority near Forty Mile. They began collecting customs on imported goods to ensure that Americans acknowledged Canadian authority. In one of his first acts, Constantine over-ruled the decision of a miner's meeting and forced the miners to accept his authority. No miners' meeting or group ever again challenged the police. Constantine reported that there were few problems with the Aboriginals or with relations between Aboriginals and non-Aboriginals. Ottawa sent twenty more and created the Yukon District of the Northwest Territories on 29 July 1895. On the eve of the gold strike, 26 years after acquiring the region, Canadian sovereignty and law were in effect on the Yukon River.

The only questions about a gold strike were when it would occur, where, and by whom. Those questions were answered on 16 August 1896, when four prospectors found sizeable quantities of nuggets and flakes in Rabbit Creek, a tributary of the Klondike River, upriver from where it joined the Yukon. It was soon appropriately re-named Bonanza Creek. The four soon-to-be famous miners were George Carmack, his wife Kate, and his two Aboriginal partners—Dawson Charlie and Skookum Jim. The mining regulations specified that claims ran 500 feet along the creek, and up the sides to the top of the ridges. After staking their claims, the happy prospectors left for Forty Mile to file them, eagerly sharing the good news with prospectors along the way. They immediately headed for Bonanza Creek, as did those in Forty Mile.

Forty Mile became a ghost town overnight as its merchants abandoned their stores and set up shop where the Klondike joined the Yukon. That instant community soon became known as Dawson City, named for George Dawson of the Geological Survey of Canada. It was an excellent location, 15 kilometres from the main gold field but with access to steam boats on the Yukon River. Merchants flooded in to provide the services the miners needed or wanted. Over the next year, dozens of hotels, saloons, theatres, restaurants, stores, and laundries sprang up, along with churches, ramshackle houses, and thousands of tents. The most famous of the entertainment establishments was the Palace Grande which could hold over 2,000 patrons. By the autumn of 1896, Dawson had a population of 1,000, jumping to 1,500 by early spring of 1897 and over 3,500 a few months later.

Within days all the land along Bonanza Creek had been claimed. Prospectors went up the small creeks nearby, and an even better find was made on one which took the name Eldorado. News of the discoveries quickly spread through the Yukon and Alaska, and hundreds of prospectors descended on the Klondike River and its tributaries. By the spring of 1897, many of the best sites had been claimed, and many miners had taken as much gold as they could carry.

The 50 claims along the Eldorado produced half a million dollars each on average, an enormous fortune at that time. In July 1897, two steamboats docked in San Francisco and Seattle with a number of happy prospectors weighed down with $1.5 million in gold. Their arrival set off the Klondike Gold Rush as thousands of miners, would-be-miners, adventurers, and "miners of miners" booked passage on any vessel heading north. Word quickly spread throughout North America and abroad, and thousands more began travelling towards the Yukon.

One major question was what route to follow. The safest was to take a steamer to the mouth of the Yukon River and book passage on a paddle wheeler going upriver to Dawson City. Though that was the slowest and most expensive route, the few paddle wheelers were quickly booked up. The fastest way into the Yukon was the fur trade route the Tlingit had guarded so jealously for a century. There were two branches. One began at Skagway, Alaska, went uphill gradually for a few kilometres, then climbed up the Chilkoot Pass on a 45 degree pathway to the summit which was in British Columbia. From there an easy path led to Lakes Bennett and Lindeman, which fed into the Yukon River. The climb to the summit could only be made on foot. Each Klondiker had about a ton of equipment and food, and it took 20 trips, each one a tremendous effort. With thousands of men climbing the pass in single file, it could take two weeks to get all of one's supplies to the top, and the Klondike Gold Rush was immortalized in a picture of an endless string of mankind struggling straight up the mountain loaded down with supplies.

The other quick route began at Dyea on the next inlet south of Skagway and took an easier climb over the White Pass. Horses and mules could be used, and the route was soon littered with the corpses of animals that had been worked to death, fallen over cliffs, or been killed after breaking their legs on the rocks. From the top of the summit an easy road led to Lakes Bennett and Lindeman. The NWMP met the Klondikers at the top of both passes, inspected supplies, and sent back those who could not prove they had enough to last a year. That policy was enacted to ensure that there would be no starvation and hence no excuse for American intervention. The NWMP collected customs duties to assert Canadian sovereignty and their own authority. They also identified undesirable personnel and denied them entry even though they did not have legal authority to do so. Around 30,000 Klondikers climbed those two passes. Edmonton hoped to cash in on the craze, and advertised itself as the gateway to the north when it was, in fact, a terrible route to follow. Two thousand men were fooled, few of whom completed the journey.

Most Klondikers arrived at the lakes too late in the season to go downstream to Dawson City. Over the winter they cut trees and built boats and rafts. On 29 May 1898, the ice went out on the river, and thousands of craft headed downstream. The 1,000 kilometre ride was smooth sailing except for two sets of rapids in Miles Canyon. A number of boats capsized and several dozen lives were lost. The NWMP immediately intervened, making up whatever rules they thought necessary and obtaining approval from Ottawa later. They inspected vessels and stopped those that were unseaworthy, forced vessels to hire employees who knew how to navigate the rapids, ensured that the boats were not overloaded, and ordered women and children to portage around the rapids. An enterprising man made a fortune by building a tramway around the rapids. Similarly, on the Chilkoot Pass someone installed a lift to carry cargo to the summit, making another fortune. When the Klondikers reached their destination, they found the rapidly expanding metropolis of Dawson City. With a population of over 30,000, it was the largest city in Canada west of Winnipeg.

Unfortunately for the Klondikers almost all of the good claims had been filed the previous year, and many of the instant millionaires had already left. For the people who "mined the miners," there were still fortunes to be made from successful prospectors who had not yet left, from those eking out a good living from the poorer claims, and from the newcomers who still hoped to make their fortunes. Many of the latter sold their supplies and left; others sought work in the stores, in transportation, or working for the miners.

The NWMP occupied a key position in this instant boom town. By the spring of 1898 there were 200 police. By summer there were 300, supported by 200 Canadian soldiers of the Yukon Field Force. As the only government officials in the region, they had almost unlimited power, and exercised almost every government function. In the absence of judges, the police could arrest, charge, sentence, and jail anyone. To be arrested by the police meant almost certain sentencing to hard labour. Geography was an ally as there were only three good routes criminals could use to escape, all of them controlled by the police. The miners themselves were allies because they needed security.

The Yukon was in effect a police state, and the police used their extraordinary authority to create a relatively peaceful environment. After defending Canadian sovereignty, their top priority was the maintenance of law and order. They did not want Dawson City to be a replica of Skagway, a town run by gangsters and notorious for murder, theft, violence, and the fleecing of outsiders. Guns were banned in Dawson City, and the police strictly enforced that ban. Robert Service's famous poem—*The Shooting of Dan McGrew*—contained the line: "Then I ducked my head and the lights went out, and two guns blazed in the night." In fact, no shots ever rang out in a Dawson saloon. A few murders were committed, and almost all the perpetrators were punished. The NWMP dealt ruthlessly with petty theft. They did not have the authority to deport undesirables, but such people were arrested, charged with some crime, and told that charges would be dropped if they left. Facing certain conviction, most took the hint.

At this time southern Canada was in the throes of a Protestant evangelical drive to perfect mankind by forcing government to treat the violation of moral values as crimes. As a consequence, alcohol, gambling, and prostitution had all been made illegal. The NWMP did not believe such laws could be enforced. They simply ignored those laws and concentrated on preventing violence, registering claims, protecting gold shipments, solving thousands of disputes over claims and access to water or timber resources, and providing basic governance. The young, male population was entertained in the saloons, dance halls and theatres, and what they did with their time and money was up to their own conscience and judgment, not that of the police or the moral crusaders down south. It was also illegal in Canada to work or enjoy public entertainment on Sundays, a law the police did enforce.

Meanwhile, at Bonanza and Eldorado the miners worked the creek beds producing a steady stream of wealth. They set up sluice boxes, shovelled the sand and gravel into the high end, and diverted creek water through them. The water washed the muck downwards, and the heavier gold flakes and nuggets settled to the bottom where they could be collected. As soon as the topsoil had been processed, the miners ran into permafrost which also contained gold. They build fires on top of the permafrost, thawed a few feet of it, and run that through the sluice boxes.

In the winter of 1897-98, miners set fires to thaw the permafrost, and piled the gravel and muck on the surface, waiting for spring when the sun would melt it again and it could be run through the sluice boxes. Permafrost was so hard that, when a vein of gold was found, the miners could follow it down to bedrock or tunnel sideways. Some prospectors found gold in the hills immediately above the creek beds, and a new wave of miners attacked the hill sides. These processes, including cutting trees and diverting water, wreaked enormous damage on the environment, damage that can still be seen. Within two years the miners had worked out most of the claims and production began to fall. The discovery of gold in Alaska in the winter of 1898-99 led to an exodus from Dawson City whose population fell from over 30,000 to 20,000 in 1901, and to half that by 1911.

Sluice boxes were not the most efficient means of extracting gold, and had in fact left millions of dollars worth of gold in the tailings and in the ground. The technology to extract that was the dredge: large machines that scoped up huge amounts of soil and washed it more thoroughly than sluice boxes could. Creeks were dammed so the dredges could float, and they ate up the soil in front of them and spewed out the waste behind, advancing from side to side until the creek bed was exhausted, and then moving slowly forward. To get at the soil farther up the hillside, hydraulic water guns blasted the soil into mud which slid down into the creeks in front of the dredges. Dredges used so much water that it had to be piped from distances of over 100 kilometres.

Dredges were expensive and required large areas of land. Companies brought them in, took over lapsed claims and bought out claims already worked over. That required a change in regulations, and Ottawa was very eager to comply. The federal government was concerned that much of the wealth was being mined by Americans who took it back to the United States. The government tried to impose a 20% royalty, but resistance was so strong that it was reduced to a 2.5% export tax. Large companies, however, could be forced to buy more expensive licences and pay larger royalties, and Canadian companies could be favoured. To no one's surprise, the licences tended to go to companies with good ties to the governing federal Liberal Party.

The most famous of these new entrepreneurs was A.N.C. Treadgold, who established the Yukon Gold Company. He received large concessions from the government, including all-important rights to timber and water. Miners in general opposed the introduction of dredges, though many were happy to sell their worked-over claims to the big companies. But they vigorously opposed the contract to Treadgold because of its size and the overly-generous terms. Local businessmen also opposed the concessions because they benefitted more from an industry based on thousands of individual miners. A number of lawsuits followed, and the concession was modified. Progress could not, however, be stopped, and within five years the gold industry shifted from an operation of thousands of individual miners to one dominated by a few companies. That is how it remained until the last dredge was shut down in 1966.

The Klondikers who arrived in the summer of 1898 soon realized that they had missed the boom. Many left but more still came, finding work on the margins of the industry or sitting in the saloons waiting for some hint as to where their futures lay. The rapid expansion in population had led the federal government to make the Yukon a separate District of the Northwest Territories in July 1895. Then in June 1898, it was made a separate Territory, a status it retained after the gold rush. The new Yukon government consisted of a Commissioner and a five-man council, both appointed by Ottawa, the councillors all being federal government officials including the Superintendent of the NWMP. The Commissioner got on with the tasks of local administration, but real power rested in Ottawa, mainly in the Department of the Interior.

The gold rush had little effect on Aboriginals. It was concentrated in the lower end of the small Klondike Valley while the Aboriginals lived throughout the vast Yukon Territory. Unlike fur traders and whalers, miners did not need help from Aboriginals, though some were hired to cut timber and there was some fraternizing with local women. Some Aboriginal people were hired as teamsters or to supply steamboats with wood, but this was part-time work which only supplemented their hunting and trapping. The missionaries did all they could to keep Aboriginals away from non-Aboriginals settlements, and the NWMP discouraged contact. When they did come to mining settlements, they were carefully segregated in their own areas some distance from the main community. Nevertheless, alcohol and disease were serious problems, and the Aboriginal population declined.

After 1899, Dawson City began to deteriorate physically while it improved morally. The latter reflected a dramatic change in demographics with more families, women and children and far fewer single men. In 1901, 1902 and especially 1904, the government cracked down on gambling, drinking, and prostitution. Declining clientele plus a new regulation making it illegal to serve liquor in dance halls forced the last one to close in 1908. The proportion of civil servants increased, and the government paradoxically erected federal buildings to serve a rapidly shrinking population.

The gold rush left a shrinking city and a great memory which merged into folklore and became part of the Canadian identity, but it did not leave any basis for diversified economic development other than the continued exploitation of gold. One permanent result of the gold rush was a vast improvement to the transportation and communications systems of the region. Between 1898 and 1900, a group of British investors eliminated the terrible climb up the Chilkoot and White Passes by building the 160-kilometre-long White Pass and Yukon Railway from Skagway to Whitehorse. It was one of the few railways built in Canada without government subsidies, and was instantly profitable. It remained so for 80 years until the government built a highway. Whitehorse flourished as the eastern terminus of the railway and the southern terminus of steamboat traffic on the Yukon. The railway made travel easy and facilitated the development of a transient, seasonal economy, with people arriving for the summer period of activity and then spending the winter down south. The quality of river transportation surged ahead to provide for the needs of almost 40,000 people. In 1901, a telegraph line was completed, and the Yukon became the first region in the North to have instant communications with the outside world, a huge leap from 1896 when word of the gold rush had to be carried by steamer to Seattle.

Chapter 5

Sovereignty, Borders, and Governance

Between 1880 and 1930, the political boundaries of the Canadian North were fixed, and Canadian sovereignty over the Arctic mainland and islands was recognized by other countries. In 1870, the new, enlarged federal colony of Canada acquired the HBC territory on the mainland, and renamed it the North-West Territories, or NWT. At that time Quebec and Ontario occupied only the northern watersheds of the St Lawrence River and the Great Lakes, a strip of land less than 200 miles wide. Everything north and west of that was included in the NWT, whose southern border with the United States was the 49th parallel. The tiny province of Manitoba was carved out of the NWT in 1870, but the vast majority of Canada's land surface consisted of the NWT, with its administrative capital soon established in Battleford and then in Regina.

Canada viewed the NWT as a territory to be exploited for the benefit of the original four provinces and as a crucial building block in creating a colony stretching from the Atlantic to the Pacific. The valuable part of the NWT, in the eyes of Ontario and Quebec, was the prairies, whose rich agricultural land could be developed through the building of a railway, which would also round out the Dominion by bringing British Columbia into the federation. Ontario and Quebec were still developing their own economies, and neither paid much attention to the lands north of the St Lawrence and the Great Lakes watersheds. Apart from the prairies, Canadians were almost completely uninterested in the rest of the NWT, content to allow the HBC to carry on with the fur trade, and happy to allow Aboriginals to live as they had for centuries. Settling the prairies and building a railway to the Pacific would strain the financial, human, and political capacity of the new Dominion to the limit, and Ottawa wanted no obligations in the NWT that would require money or attention.

Britain, however, was not content simply to transfer HBC land to Canada. Because of exploration by British subjects, it had the best claim of any country to sovereignty over the Arctic islands. There did not appear to be much economic value in them. Possession was becoming somewhat troublesome, and sovereignty became an issue because explorers, whalers, and miners from a variety of countries continued to pass through the waters and over the islands. In 1874, Britain asked Canada if it was interested in taking control of the islands. Ottawa did not want them either, but, like Britain, it wanted even less for some other country to own them, especially the United States. Reluctantly, therefore, it agreed in principle to the transfer.

Three years later Britain pressed again, and both parties in the House of Commons in Ottawa supported a resolution accepting possession of the Arctic islands. The British transfer, however, was done by an administrative Order-in-Council of 1 September 1880, rather than by a more transparent and legally meaningful Parliamentary resolution. Inasmuch as the islands had been British, they were now Canadian, but the borders were deliberately left vague in the British documents. Even the HBC said it did not know exactly what was being transferred. Canada's newfound sovereignty was very questionable for a number of reasons. No one knew how many islands there were. The United States had legitimate claims, but London did not tell the Canadians about that. Britain's claim rested on discovery, but discovery was just the first step to asserting sovereignty over any newly-discovered land. To make a claim firm, the claimant had to establish a presence through settlement, use, or administration. Britain had made no attempt to do so, and explorers and whalers from a number of countries were using the islands. The situation was further complicated by the fact that until 1931, Canada was technically a British colony and not a sovereign country, so until 1931, any negotiations with foreign countries had to be conducted by London.

Like Britain, Canada did little to assert its sovereignty over the islands, and foreign nationals continued to search for the Northwest Passage, explore the islands, look for minerals, trade with the Inuit, and hunt and travel over land, water, and ice. Fortunately, none of their national governments claimed sovereignty. In effect, the islands remained a "no man's land," and in the 1880s and 1890s, that was quite satisfactory to Canada and to the various countries whose nationals were active in the Arctic.

By the turn of the century, however, that situation was changing. Explorers from Norway wanted their government to claim the islands they were discovering and using. Americans were exploring, using the islands, and even attempting to export minerals. One American, Robert Peary, made northern Ellesmere Island the base for his attempts to be the first man to reach the North Pole, and his party almost denuded the region of wildlife. Peary wanted to claim the region for the United States, but Washington did not support him. Whalers continued their fishing and fur trading activities in disregard of Canadian law, which was not difficult as there were no Canadian officials anywhere near the islands.

In 1896, a new, strong, and aggressive Liberal Government replaced a tired and divided Conservative dynasty, and brought energy and imagination to a host of issues including the Arctic. Its attitude was strongly influenced by the development of whaling in the western Arctic, where Americans occupied Herschel Island, and to the fact that by the mid-1890s there were over 1,000 American miners in the Yukon. Indeed, American ships were surveying Arctic islands and giving official names to the geographical features. Ottawa was also well aware by then that the British documents transferring sovereignty were problematic. Ottawa sent the NWMP to the Klondike and Herschel Island, their top priority being the assertion of sovereignty. In 1897, Ottawa finally claimed sovereignty over the entire Arctic archipelago, incorporated the islands into the NWT administratively, and sent expeditions to plant the Canadian flag on the islands themselves.

The federal government reinforced the claim by establishing a NWMP detachment at Pond Inlet on Baffin Island. More and more NWMP were sent into the islands to raise the flag, build posts, visit the Inuit, check foreigners, collect customs revenue, and undertake long patrols by boat in summer and dog sled in winter. They engaged in activities specifically designed to assert sovereignty, such as imposing Canadian law on Aboriginals and stamping letters to prove that the postal system in the region was Canadian. Some of the detachments such as the one established on Ellesmere Island in the 1920s had no purpose other than asserting sovereignty because there were no people to police.

The activities of the NWMP were backed by expeditions specifically designed to lay claim to the islands, by erecting cairns saying the islands were Canadian, by discovering and claiming new islands, and by informing foreign ship captains that the region was under Canadian law. The government purchased a ship and hired Joseph Bernier, a seasoned navigator. Between 1904 and 1911, he undertook four expeditions to the North to assert Canadian ownership. One of the first deliberate acts of the federal government was to require whalers to obtain licences from Canadian authorities.

The ambiguity over sovereignty was not ended by the actions of Canadian police or explorers, because a country only has sovereignty over land if other countries recognize it, and the United States, Norway and Denmark clearly did not. In the 1920s, the American government supported an expedition to Ellesmere Island. It suspended that support after Ottawa complained, but it still refused to recognize Canadian claims to the territory. In 1926, Ottawa created the Arctic Islands Game Preserve including all the Arctic islands, and sent police patrols to demonstrate that Canada occupied the whole territory. On the other hand, Norway, Denmark, and the United States took no steps to prove that they occupied any islands. Finally, Britain obtained recognition of Canadian sovereignty from those three governments.

In the meantime the western border of the NWT was established when the Yukon was made a separate territory in 1898, and the southern border was fixed when Saskatchewan and Alberta were established in 1905 and Manitoba was enlarged in 1912. Saskatchewan and Alberta extended northwards to the 60th parallel so that roughly half their area was in Canada's North, and the NWT was reduced accordingly. Manitoba's northern border was not changed in 1905, so the oldest and proudest prairie province suddenly found itself with half the territory of the two new ones. Negotiations over the northern border of Manitoba dragged on for years, and in 1912, the new federal Conservative administration extended Manitoba's border to the 60th, another loss of territory for the NWT. At the same time it extended the northern borders of Ontario and Quebec to Hudson Bay and Hudson Strait, so that Quebec's borders reached well north of the 60th parallel. With these changes and the successful assertion of sovereignty, the political and administrative borders of the Canadian North were finally determined. Geographically, ethnically, and economically, however, the North had been divided, with one third of it administered by six provinces and the separate British colony of Newfoundland.

The creation of the territory of the Yukon and of the provinces of Saskatchewan and Alberta necessitated changes in the way the Canadian North was governed. In 1898, the Yukon had been given a Commissioner and a five-man Council, all of them federal officials. After the gold rush and the departure of most of the Americans, it was given representative government in the form of an advisory assembly of ten, five of them elected. By 1908, all were elected. In 1902, the Yukon was given one Member of Parliament, and its MPs established good reputations defending the interests of their constituents. The franchise for all these elections included all adult men with British citizenship and twelve months residence, thus weeding out Americans and transients. As the population of the Yukon shrank over the next four decades, government was correspondingly diminished. Positions were eliminated, the remaining officials took on more and more responsibilities, and in 1911, the Legislative Council was reduced from ten to three.

Before 1905, local government of the Northwest Territories was administered from Regina, though power over important issues such as public lands and natural resources was wielded by the Department of the Interior in Ottawa. When Saskatchewan and Alberta were created, the territorial government in Regina was abolished and its limited powers transferred to Ottawa. NWMP Comptroller Frederick White took on the added duties of Commissioner as a part-time job. His main functions were distributing education grants to churches and issuing liquor licences. He was to be assisted by a Council consisting of four senior federal officials, but these were not appointed until 1921. In fact, each Department with interests in the North exercised its responsibilities independently, and when the Council was finally appointed, it was really an inter-departmental coordinating group that had no staff and met only once a year. It inherited all the regulations the old administration in Regina had passed, changed a few, but passed no new ones for decades.

In 1921, 25 bureaucrats from Ottawa were transferred to Fort Smith on the Mackenzie River, giving the NWT its first resident government since 1905.

Ottawa continued to make all the major decisions and often did not inform let alone consult its satellite government at Fort Smith. As far as Ottawa was concerned, the NWT was essentially self-governing since the vast majority of inhabitants were Aboriginals who continued to govern themselves as they always had. Unlike the First Nations, the Inuit did not fall under the jurisdiction of the Indian Act and had, for all intents and purposes, the same rights as other Canadians. The RCMP, however, often treated the Inuit like First Nations by, for example, applying liquor laws under the Indian Act. There was almost no criticism of this government except when it tried to raise taxes. Business interests constantly pressed it for better infrastructure, but its budget was very limited. This system of government hardly changed until the 1960s.

Chapter 6

Police, Missionaries, and Economic Development

Two groups, the RNWMP (RCMP after 1921) and Christian missionaries actually provided most of the governance of the Yukon and NWT. The NWMP was originally sent to the North to assert sovereignty and maintain law and order. As the only government agents in the North, they also carried out a wide range of activities, including collecting customs and revenue, registering land and mining titles, handling the post and telegraph, distributing welfare, and spying on American organizations. A particularly important role was the enforcement of game laws as excessive hunting had reduced some Aboriginals to starvation.

Once a year the RCMP delivered liquor to those with permits to import it, and then dealt with the consequences of the resulting binge. They fought forest fires, dealt with floods, and spent less than half their time on police duties. Officers had great discretion and often ignored minor infractions, partly because bringing people to trial over great distances was extremely expensive in both time and money, and could be very dangerous. The extraordinary powers held by RCMP officers appear to have been exercised with considerable caution and common sense. They made regular visits to remote communities so that everyone knew they would return the following year to investigate crimes and complaints. The image of the Mounties as fearless, forceful, resourceful, and successful became an important element in Canada's Northern identity, and indeed in the Canadian identity

Missionaries wanted the police to devote much of their time to the imposition of moral values which had become law in the provinces. The RCMP did not believe the missionaries' views of sex and marriage could or even should be enforced. The RCMP were also well aware of the difficulty of treating as criminal activities Aboriginals had always viewed as acceptable. Even murder was treated differently. In 1912, two Inuit killed two explorers. The police concluded that they had acted in self defence, and released them. One year later, two Inuit killed two priests. The police concluded that the priests had threatened them, and the two men were imprisoned for only two years. Then, two Inuit charged with murder killed the policeman who had captured them. They were re-captured, tried and hanged, the first Inuit to suffer the death penalty in Canada. It was more common, however, for the RCMP to protect Aboriginals. The most famous example was that of the "mad trapper"—Albert Johnson. He began trapping illegally near Fort McPherson, and interfered with local trap lines. When the police went to investigate, Johnson shot at them and then fled.

That touched off a two-month man-hunt in which numerous police assisted by aircraft could not catch a man they knew nothing about except that he was capable of out-running them while living off the land. He was finally cornered and killed, but not before he had killed one policeman, seriously wounded two civilians, and dominated the Canadian news for weeks on end.

The other major European presence in the North was that of the missionaries, who, in effect, were also government agents. Even before Canada acquired the NWT, the Anglican and Roman Catholic churches decided that the population in the North should be Christianized. Around 1850, Catholics and Anglicans launched major missionary movements in the North. They began competing for the souls of the inhabitants, with both organizations building churches in the same communities and attacking each other with accusations, slanders, and rumours. Unfortunately for the Protestants, the competition heavily favoured the Catholics. The latter had an order of brothers—the Oblates—who were sworn to chastity, poverty, and a life of missionary work no matter how difficult that might be. They were willing, indeed eager, to live with the local population and learn their languages, often spending their entire careers with one group.

In contrast, Anglicans saw missionary activity in the North as an early stage in a career to be spent in the south. The Anglicans had difficulty attracting their best ministers to the North, and those that came rarely learned local languages. They often preferred to live at the HBC posts, attempting to maintain a southern lifestyle. They wanted the Aboriginals to understand Christianity and not just perform Christian rites, and they wanted to change their allegedly primitive culture. The Anglicans thus combined more ambitious goals with a far less effective effort. A geographic pattern emerged, with the Catholics dominant in the more populous Mackenzie Valley and the Anglicans more numerous in the Yukon and the eastern Arctic. By 1896, 3,500 Aboriginals were registered as Catholics, fewer than 1,000 as Anglicans.

Nominally, the Aboriginal people were converted to Christianity and adopted many of the outward manifestations of that religion. It is not clear, however, how deeply their conversions went, and they maintained many of their ancient beliefs and practices. This did not necessarily involve contradictions because their spiritualism was an all-embracing concept that placed people in the context of their entire environment. Christianity, which was more narrowly focussed, could be fitted into that cosmos, especially if it was limited to Sunday worship.

In Medieval Europe churches provided education, health, and welfare, and that system was carried to the New World. In the mid-nineteenth century, provincial governments began asserting control over these issues, but the federal government preferred to leave education, health, and welfare in the hands of the churches. The churches, in turn, were willing to build and operate schools and hospitals because such institutions were essential instruments in their Christianizing and civilizing missions. The federal government therefore delegated its responsibility, or perhaps abdicated it, to churches, offering them subsidies to help with their costs.

The churches built day and residential schools. Day schools provided for the children of families who lived in or near larger communities part or most of the year. Residential schools were provided for children who lived long distances from communities, the children sometimes living at the schools permanently for years. The schools adopted the curriculum of southern Canada because they were preparing the students for work and integration into mainstream society and because they wanted to replace their culture with the supposedly superior European civilization. The curriculum was occasionally augmented with practical skills such as carpentry, hygiene, and cooking.

Overall, the schools failed in their main goals. Employment opportunities were limited, and employers were reluctant to hire Aboriginals even if they could read and write. By taking children out of their culture and exposing them to western civilization during their formative years, the schools produced pupils who, when they returned to their communities, lacked the skills needed to contribute to those communities. After years of instruction that denigrated their culture, they were uncomfortable with Aboriginal ways. They often forgot much of what they had learned at school without learning the aspects of their own culture. Instead of exhibiting the best of two civilizations, they came to represent the worst, incapable of functioning properly in either. That was the beginning of a tragic descent from pride and self-sufficiency into dependency, idleness, alcohol, and family violence, societal characteristics that were not normal in Aboriginal communities.

In the North, the First World War I had little impact on Aboriginals, but many men of British background quickly volunteered to save King and Empire. In fact, the North had the highest per capita enlistment in Canada, as well as the greatest per capita contribution to voluntary organizations. The experience of Northerner troops was put to good use in forestry, while Aboriginals distinguished themselves, particularly as snipers. The war increased dramatically the demand for minerals but, at the same time, took away much of the labour force needed to extract them, so mineral production increased in value while the volume of exports actually declined.

The economy was relatively stagnant between the First and Second World Wars. The fur trade remained the major economic activity, but it suffered from huge fluctuations in price and demand and from over-trapping. Non-aboriginal trappers used better equipment and would often trap out an area and then move on to another. Others, such as miners and tourists, hunted and fished for food and sport, and the continuous decline in animal life left Aboriginals more and more vulnerable to starvation and disease. The high expectations for oil and gas development in the Mackenzie Delta did not materialize, though some oil was produced at Norman Wells. Gold mining continued at a modest rate in the Yukon. Paradoxically, mining improved during the great Depression, a particularly important discovery being a rich deposit of silver and pitchblende near Great Bear Lake. Pitchblende produced radium which was used for fighting cancer and making instrument dials.

While mining did not produce an economic boom, it did lead to major improvements in transportation. River transportation underwent considerable modernization with the introduction of oil and diesel powered boats and the use of trucks and tractor trains on ice highways in winter. The main revolution in transportation, however, was the introduction of airplanes which reduced travel time from weeks to hours and took prospectors, workers, and mining equipment into remote areas. Bush pilots such as "Wop" May became famous for their exploits, especially flying sick and injured people to hospitals. Regular passenger service was initiated between Yellowknife and Edmonton, and regular air mail replaced delivery by dog sled.

Many Aboriginal people were relatively prosperous during the 1920s due to the high price of furs, though they suffered from diseases and became increasingly dependent on western food, clothing, and equipment. Their condition then deteriorated rapidly during the Depression. It accelerated urbanization because many Aboriginal people built houses near trading posts and larger communities so they could receive food. The federal government, however, made it difficult for them to obtain welfare, and spent half as much on them as on other Canadians. Demographics told the story as the total Aboriginal population fell between the two World Wars.

One major attempt to deal with declining wildlife stocks involved the introduction of reindeer. Three thousand were purchased in Alaska, and herded over to the Mackenzie Delta where caribou had become extinct. The reindeer drive took six years, and several smaller herds were moved farther east, providing meat and hides for the local population. At the same time Ottawa made major efforts to protect wildlife, including tougher licensing laws, limited hunting seasons, fewer licences, and the exclusion of non-Aboriginals from trapping in the eastern half of the NWT. Two parks were established to protect wildlife: Wood Buffalo Park along the Alberta border in 1922 and Thelon Game Sanctuary east of Great Slave Lake in 1927. The problem of over-hunting and trapping was so serious that the RCMP were empowered to search anything anytime to enforce game laws.

It was never the intention of the federal government to negotiate treaties with the Aboriginals in the North. Treaties were designed primarily to extinguish First Nations claims to agricultural land, but there was little agricultural land in the NWT and the Yukon, and Ottawa did not want to establish reserves on land that might contain gold or other minerals. In addition, Ottawa had no intention of assuming the type of financial obligations that were needed to induce prairie First Nations to sign treaties. As far as Ottawa was concerned, the original population could continue to live as they had for centuries, hopefully without causing any problems or requiring any attention or expense.

The Yukon gold rush brought heightened economic activity to the Mackenzie Valley, prompting Ottawa to "negotiate" an agreement. Treaty #8 was essentially dictated by government officials in 1899, and it became clear later that the First Nations did not understand what they had acquired, surrendered, or retained. The Treaty gave them an enormous reserve of 325,000 square miles straddling the NWT-Alberta border. Their rights to land outside that area were extinguished, and they thought, incorrectly, that they had become eligible for government assistance. They retained the right to hunt, fish, and trap on the reserve. Later, when Ottawa passed laws restricting hunting for conservation reasons, the courts said that federal law superseded treaty rights, which implied that the treaty actually gave no permanent protection at all.

When oil was discovered at Norman Wells, the federal government decided to extinguish land claims in order to open the lower Mackenzie Delta for economic development. Like Treaty #8, Treaty #11 of 1921 was more of a federal dictate than a negotiated document. The First Nations ceded their title to land and privileges in return for land grants of 640 acres per family and annual monetary grants, and they were paid to sign. They also believed they had been promised health and welfare services. The area reserved for them was enormous—620,000 square kilometres. The First Nations reserved the right to hunt, fish, and trap on the lands ceded, but the federal government retained the power to restrict those rights should it choose to do so.

Chapter 7

The Second World War

The Second World War brought profound change to the Yukon, considerable change to the Mackenzie Valley, and some developments in the rest of the NWT. As war clouds gathered in Asia and Europe in the 1930s, both Canada and the United States believed they could remain isolated from another great war. The actual outbreak of war in Europe in September, 1939, changed all that. In the North, people responded as they had in 1914, producing a higher proportion of recruits and more voluntary fundraising than in other provinces. Once more, Aboriginal people volunteered in large numbers and made their presence felt as snipers. Across the Atlantic, England was not prepared for war, and both Canada and the United States realized it would need massive assistance. That required more and better airfields and weather stations in the eastern Arctic.

Then on 7 December 1941, Japan attacked the American naval base at Pearl Harbour, Hawaii. The dream of neutrality went up in smoke along with a considerable portion of the Pacific fleet, and the United States and Canada suddenly faced the prospect of Japanese attacks along the west coast. Neither government was prepared, and the response was panic, one manifestation being the decision to build a road to Alaska, a distance of 2,400 kilometres beyond existing roads. Politicians in the Yukon, Alaska, and British Columbia had long advocated such a highway, and the Japanese threat to the west coast gave powerful support to the concept. The American military, however, concluded that the enormous investment was not justified by the threat. Politicians over-ruled the military mainly to show the public that something was being done to protect them.

Politicians in Ottawa were very sceptical about the advisability of building such a road. Politically, however, it was not desirable to challenge American wartime demands. Accordingly, the Canadian government approved the American plan, and gave the United States permission to build the highway through Canadian territory, wherever it wanted. It was to be entirely at American expense, with ownership reverting to Canada six months after the war ended. Americans would have full control of every aspect of construction, and their servicemen would come under American law and police at the construction sites and bases.

Little of the relevant land surface had been surveyed, and knowledge about building roads in such terrain was not good. There were three possible routes: along the coast, through the mountains of north central British Columbia, or east of the Rockies. Military planners chose the third. The US Army Corps of

Engineers began work in the late spring of 1942, with a six month deadline. Aircraft and local people were used to survey routes, and work began simultaneously in both directions from four construction centres. The US Army quickly brought in 10,000 soldiers and 10,000 civilians, four times the entire population of the Yukon. Thousands of pieces of equipment were shipped to Skagway, up the railway to Whitehorse, and on to the construction sites.

Crews, equipment, and supplies were flown in to bridge sites so that road-building crews would not be held up by rivers. Bulldozers scraped the forest and brush away and levelled the ground. Engineers learned how to deal with permafrost, namely by building a layer of insulation over it so it would not melt with the weight of the road and traffic, and then building the road on top of the insulation. The initial goal was to build a military road 16 feet wide, with many temporary bridges, steep hills, and sharp turns. Americans took control of the Skagway to Whitehorse railway, gave preference to freight over passengers, and to American supplies over Canadian goods. The trains ran virtually non-stop causing a serious deterioration in the railway. To provide communications, a phone line was built alongside the Highway. The low construction standards allowed the Army to complete the Alaska Highway on time, one of the most amazing engineering feats in the history of North America.

As it turned out, there was no threat of a Japanese invasion, Japanese submarines never threatened shipping, and the United States abandoned the concept of bombing Japan from Alaskan airfields. The Highway was useful for supplying airfields, and a massive amount of war materiel was shipped to the Soviet Union by air. But the Highway was not, in fact, needed for the defence of North America, and represented a massive diversion of men, money and equipment from more useful projects. Civilian contractors then replaced the Army Corps of Engineers. Their job was to replace temporary bridges, deal with the steep hills and sharp turns, widen the road, and make it an all-year, all-weather civilian road. They worked on those improvements for two years, but their budgets were gradually reduced. The specifications were down-graded, and by 1945, the road was still not suitable for civilian use. The US government asked Ottawa to take over maintenance and to take ownership before the agreed date, but Ottawa refused both requests.

The construction of the road transformed the entire region through which it passed. The US Army hired local workers, and Canadian mines and companies found themselves with serious labour shortages. Mines had never hired many Aboriginal workers, but now they had no choice. Even so, mineral production declined. American spending power touched off inflation. Americans were allowed to hunt and fish, and they quickly exhausted the local forests and rivers. They sometimes hunted purely for sport, leaving carcasses for the wolves while Aboriginal people went hungry. The federal government responded by banning hunting between the Highway and the Alaskan and BC borders, an area that became Kluane National Park and was eventually declared a World Heritage Site by UNESCO.

The second major war-induced development was the building of a 1,000 kilometre long oil pipeline from Norman Wells to a new refinery in Whitehorse, a project known as the Canol Pipeline. It was very expensive shipping oil and gasoline up the coast and over the railway to Whitehorse, and some military officials in Washington concluded that they could take advantage of the small oil field that had been discovered at Norman Wells. The generals ignored the negative views of Imperial Oil, and did not seek advice from the few people who had some relevant expertise. The one Canadian involved in decision-making objected so vehemently to the ill-conceived scheme that the United States went over his head to obtain approval from the federal Cabinet.

At a cost similar to that of the Alaska Highway, thousands of workers and millions of dollars worth of equipment and supplies were brought in. Imperial Oil was ordered to drill hundreds of new wells throughout the Mackenzie and Liard River Valleys, wells which added little to production. A path was bulldozed through the forest, and the pipeline lain on top of the permafrost. When oil flowed through it, the permafrost melted, and the pipe often sank and broke. The oil was high in paraffin, which clogged the pipe. The project was so badly designed and managed that the work force did not take it seriously. Morale was abysmal, and workmanship terrible.

It took two years to build the pipeline, and cost over five times the original estimate. When products began flowing from the refinery in Whitehorse, they cost 25 times as much as the expensive ones imported by ship and railway. At war's end neither Ottawa nor any private companies were interested in acquiring it. Both the pipeline and refinery were dismantled and the parts shipped back south. Equipment that could not be shipped was left to rust, buildings abandoned, and an ugly scar left across the landscape including pools of oil that caused environmental damage for years. The Canol Pipeline was one of the worst economic decisions made in North America during the war and, like the Alaska Highway, diverted resources from more useful projects.

The presence of such a huge work force of single men for the two projects produced problems of prostitution, venereal disease, unwanted pregnancies, and alcohol abuse. New types of diseases struck defenceless Aboriginals, and their death rate soared. New layers of segregation were added to society. To reduce the drain of labour from Canadian companies and businesses, the federal government asked American companies to hire only Americans, and Canadians who were hired were paid less than half the wages of Americans. Canadians, in effect, were discriminated against in their own country, and by their own government. In the American work force, Blacks were segregated from Whites and discriminated against. Canadian communities continued to ensure that Aboriginal people lived separately and entered towns and cities under strict rules.

The Canadian government accepted that Americans would police the highway and pipeline. Ottawa also agreed that American servicemen would come under American law on their bases, but they soon came under American law everywhere as did American civilians working on military projects. Ottawa did not send adequate police to enforce Canadian law. In fact, it sent roughly one tenth as many police as it had during the Yukon gold rush. The town of Whitehorse did not provide sufficient police even to control traffic. That was a threat to the project, and Americans stepped into the vacuum, attempting to maintain law and order in Whitehorse. When Americans caused trouble, American Military Police sent them home before the RCMP could investigate.

The population of Whitehorse exploded from around 700 in 1941 to 10,000 in 1943, 80% American. Servicemen were provided quarters by their government, while civilians crowded into shanty and tent towns. Water and sewage became serious health problems, and Americans built a water treatment plant, connected it to American facilities throughout the town, and allowed Canadians to tap into it. Whitehorse was forced to build a new sewage system and expand schools and hospitals. Canadians complained of American arrogance and high-handedness; Americans complained of Canadian incompetence and indifference. There was ample evidence to support both sets of complaints. Whitehorse's growth was at Dawson City's expense. A number of businesses moved, and by war's end Whitehorse had five times the population of the older community and even better transportation links to the rest of the world.

The same problems played out on the larger theatre. Ottawa paid little attention to what the Americans were doing across the Arctic. That, however, was not what the public was told. Press releases announced projects as joint when in fact Canada had no involvement in them. Americans decided where to build airports, side roads, and weather stations without even informing federal or local authorities. The first some communities knew of some project was when bulldozers began levelling the ground. By 1943, there were 33,000 Americans in the Canadian North, vastly outnumbering the adult Canadian population.

Americans talked openly of their involvement in future resource development. The American Senate mused about deriving post-war benefits from all the investment. The facilities built on some air bases exceeded military requirements, airports were built that were not needed by the military, and weather bases with landing strips grew into full-fledged airports. Canadian civil servants in the North reported their concerns, but no one in Ottawa seemed to care. No federal cabinet ministers visited the area, and the first important outside visit was that of the British High Commissioner to Canada—Malcolm MacDonald.

He informed Prime Minister Mackenzie King that the huge American presence and their activities and attitudes were a serious threat to Canada's control of its North.

Ottawa responded with minimal effort. A year after MacDonald submitted his recommendation and well after most of the important decisions had been made, Major General W.W. Foster was appointed as special liaison officer. From then on the Americans were to inform General Foster of decisions, but he and the federal government did not have an input into those decisions or a veto over them. A joint economic committee that had given Americans a voice in economic development was abolished. Ottawa's lackadaisical approach was an oddity in a war which saw the federal government and bureaucracy grow by leaps and bounds and take control of the Canadian economy. Half a century earlier the federal government had taken bold, decisive, and expensive measures to ensure Canadian control of the Yukon gold rush, but it now let foreigners do what they wanted across the entire Arctic. One of Ottawa's few achievements in asserting sovereignty was the voyage of the RCMP ship St Roch from Vancouver to Halifax and back, the first ship to sail the Northwest Passage west to east and the first to make a return trip.

War's end brought another irritant which left lasting and bitter memories. Much of the equipment used to build the highway and the pipeline could not economically be shipped back to the United States. Supplies needed by a workforce of thousands were piled up in warehouses. Selling clothing, bedding, food, tools, stationery, and furniture at bargain-basement prices would have adverse effects on local business, so Ottawa prevented such sales. As a consequence, the Americans burned warehouses full of supplies while Northerners looked on in disbelief, and in some cases, stole goods before they went up in flames. Not enough spare parts had been brought in to maintain all the equipment, so trucks and heavy equipment were often abandoned when they broke down. The departure of the Americans left thousands of vehicles, whose parts might still be of use but whose frames became ugly, rusting reminders of projects built with little regard to need or cost.

In the eastern and northern Arctic the American war effort produced airfields and weather stations, all under full American control. Although the federal government discouraged the practice and in some cases forbade it, some Aboriginal workers were hired. Small Aboriginal communities grew up around facilities at Frobisher Bay and on Southampton Island. While the salaries and access to consumer goods were welcome, these communities faced the same social problems as those along the Alaska Highway, problems of uncontrolled access to alcohol, venereal disease, and unwanted pregnancies. Before the war, most Inuit lived as they had for centuries; by 1945, their lifestyles and culture had been permanently altered. They had finally become dependent on Canadian society, and their numbers declined significantly.

By 1945, the Americans were happy to leave the Canadian North and most Northern Canadians were happy to see them go. Washington requested an extension of the joint defence agreements, but Ottawa refused. Their departure partly solved the threat they had posed to Canadian sovereignty. Ottawa took control of the Alaska Highway and sent Army engineers and later civilians to maintain it. While building it had taken six months, turning it into a road usable by civilians took three more years. Unfortunately it was in the wrong place, because the main economic zone was still the capital at Dawson City and the mining community of Mayo, and neither was linked to the outside world by road until 1955. In a belated move to assert sovereignty, Ottawa bought the 28 American airports and 56 weather stations, thus acquiring a crucial element in the northern transportation and communications systems. It took over the phone line and other facilities built along the Highway. The Americans left behind dozens of access roads, wharves, docks, warehouses, housing, electricity plants, water and sewage plants, hospitals, and hundreds of vehicles, airplanes and boats. The war also bequeathed a crucial legacy—southern Canada and its government had finally discovered the North.

Chapter 8

Slow Development, 1945-1965

As the Second World War drew to a close, fears grew that the curtailment of military spending would plunge the North back into the Depression of the 1930s. That seemed likely when the population of Whitehorse fell from 10,000 to 3,600. A combination of factors, however, resulted in continued growth. Indeed, the end of the war marked one of the most important watersheds in the history of the North. Military spending continued when new threats emerged. The Canadian public had rediscovered the North, and demanded more government action on protecting sovereignty, looking after Aboriginal peoples, and promoting development. The federal government now accepted a much larger role in developing the economy and the public had grown used to a far higher level of taxation. For the first time ever, the North was under a federal government that wanted to govern it properly, develop its economy, use it to protect the rest of Canada, and make it a lot more equal. This time the government had the money to implement new policies in these fields.

As soon as Germany was defeated, the two main allies, the United States and the Soviet Union, began competing for regional and world dominance. The shortest route to attack each other lay over the North Pole, and the Canadian North became the main potential battleground. To identify any approaching Soviet bombers, the United States decided to establish several rings of radar stations. Canada fully agreed with the strategy, and built two lines of radar stations across the continent. The United States built the third, the Distant Early Warning (DEW) Line, from Greenland to Alaska. The Canadian public was never fully informed of the extent of American activities or the degree to which they operated under exclusive American control. Press releases announced that such projects were "joint," and downplayed the military aspects while highlighting the civilian benefits.

The construction of 41 radar stations required massive and expensive investment in buildings and equipment and more airfields, weather stations, roads, and harbours. It was agreed that Canadian companies would obtain a considerable portion of the contracts. This time, Ottawa made clear that Canadian law applied on Canadian soil. Once more, the federal government discouraged the Americans from hiring Inuit or fraternizing with them. Once more, such rules could not be fully enforced, and Inuit often moved to the radar bases where they obtained jobs and came in close contact with the American lifestyle and consumer goods.

Another aspect of American strategy was the capacity to retaliate against a Soviet attack with massive air strikes. As part of a network of air bases called the Strategic Air Command or SAC, the Americans built a huge air base at Frobisher Bay. By the time these facilities were completed, new technology rendered them obsolete because Intercontinental Ballistic Missiles (ICBMs) could fly across the Arctic in minutes and were tracked by satellites rather than radar. The US closed its SAC base at Frobisher in 1964, wiping out half the town's economy, and the radar bases closed in the mid-1960s. For two decades after the Second World War, however, military spending provided a sustained and substantial economic stimulus, and it left behind a massive infrastructure.

More important in changing the North was the fact that new attitudes developed within the federal bureaucracy and Cabinet during the Second World War. One was that Canada should become a welfare state, and that the federal government should lead the way. The first new program was the Mothers' Allowance or Family Allowance, a payment of five dollars per month for each child under 16. At the time that was a substantial amount, and it brought many Aboriginal peoples into the cash economy for the first time. The Family Allowance was soon followed by old age pensions and various welfare programs for those in need.

The policy was applied universally and equitably for most Canadians, but for Aboriginal peoples, it was made conditional on them sending their children to school. One result was that many of them did. Aboriginal families often moved to established communities so their children could attend day school. They also gained access to better health facilities, and the possibility of work. Those from more remote areas sent their children to residential schools. By 1958, half the Aboriginal children were going to school, a figure that climbed to 90% a decade later.

A second provision was even more discriminatory. Most Canadian mothers received a cheque, but Aboriginal mothers received vouchers for a list of specific items they could obtain at HBC stores. The assumptions behind this provision were that the bureaucrats in Ottawa knew what families needed, and that Aboriginal women would squander the allowance if it came as cash. That paternalistic attitude ignored the fact that for centuries Aboriginal people had traded furs for the things they needed. It ignored the fact that such micromanagement of lives could not be enforced. It also ignored the fact that paternalism destroys responsibility, self-reliance, self-confidence, and self-esteem. The program helped create a vicious circle in the North in which the more welfare the government provided, the more it was needed.

Health was another new, major, and extremely important focus of federal government programming. The policy until 1945 had been to do the absolute minimum, and to meet needs on a reactive and restricted basis. The condition of Aboriginal peoples had been deteriorating, and their numbers actually declined during the war. In 1947, responsibility for their health was transferred from the Department of Indian Affairs to the Department of Health and Welfare. It immediately sent large numbers of doctors, dentists, and nurses, one result of which was to confirm that a huge proportion of the population was suffering from tuberculosis. Those infected were sent to local hospitals, which were quickly overwhelmed by the numbers, and then to hospitals in the south.

The government's newfound concern for Aboriginal peoples was heightened when stories of starvation began to appear, particularly from The Barrens in the eastern Arctic. Throughout the North, over-hunting had led to a steady decline in the stock of wildlife, and lean years were increasingly intense and frequent. A Canadian author—Farley Mowat—published *The People of the Deer* which brought national and international attention to the crisis. That attention shamed governments and private organizations into a heightened level of activity. People were moved from The Barrens to Hudson Bay, and the RCMP began distributing food. Throughout the North, hospitals were built, modernized, or expanded, more medical services were made available, and the general level of health began to improve. The birth rate had always been high, and the reduced death rate produced a rapid increase in population, possibly the first such increase since Europeans came to the North.

Another federal program to deal with starvation became quite controversial. Ottawa decided to move Inuit from Ungava, Cape Dorset and Pond Inlet where wildlife was inadequate, to Craig Harbour, Resolute, Dundas Harbour, and Grise Fiord where game was more abundant. The federal bureaucrats had not done their homework and did not make adequate preparations for the moves. The Inuit from Quebec were quite unsuited to the high Arctic, game was not as plentiful as thought, and weather conditions made hunting more difficult. Several of these groups had to be moved, sometimes several times. The federal government had a second and perhaps more important motive for the relocation, namely to reinforce Canada's claim to sovereignty by physically occupying previously uninhabited regions. When this became known years later, it was seen as a scandal, and in the 1990s, Ottawa was forced to pay compensation to the affected groups. It refused, however, to apologize, and the forced moves marked a bitter episode in Ottawa's mishandling of problems in the North.

The government's new attitudes, growing population, the movement of Aboriginal peoples from the land to communities, and the effects of the Mothers' Allowance produced a crisis in education. It had been delegated to the churches, but they were overwhelmed by the rising number of students. The federal government was forced to hire more and more teachers, many of whom did not appreciate local culture and remained in the North only for short periods. The government built more residential schools and over 50 smaller ones in scattered communities. The schools were secularized in a relatively short period of time, but continued to use a curriculum suitable for southern Canada rather than the North.

Secularization allowed Ottawa to put more emphasis on its effort to use education to assimilate the people to "Canadian" culture." It became increasingly clear that residential schools were a failure. Protests and criticism of them mounted, and they were phased out and replaced with day schools, which in turn accelerated the movement of whole families from the land to established communities, moves that did as much as the schools to "Canadianize" the local population. Gradually local teachers replaced ones from the south. They were not only more acceptable, but formed a more stable work force. Instead of punishing Aboriginal students for speaking their dialects, schools began teaching local languages and culture. Texts were translated into local dialects. The graduates of these schools were increasingly successful in obtaining full-time jobs with government and other mainstream economic sectors. They also started to provide more effective leadership for the voicing of grievances.

Urbanization was one of the greatest changes in the post-war North. In 1940, hardly any Inuit lived near new settlements. Three decades later almost all of them lived in or near communities, and the North was the most heavily urbanized part of Canada, counting towns and villages as urban. Successful urbanization and integration were different matters, however. While federal policies attracted Aboriginal peoples to communities, few preparations were made to receive them. Civil servants in Ottawa were so certain of their wisdom that they selected sites for communities without consulting either local people or the bureaucrats in the territorial governments. Civil servants designed houses without consultation or understanding of the North or the culture. People often refused to live in such houses and communities, preferring to stay in shanty towns nearby. They were close enough for access to schools, government services and stores, too far away for access to water and sewage, and their housing was substantially inferior.

It is difficult to evaluate whether the North became more or less segregated after the Second World War. Mining companies built enclosed "southern communities" with all the necessary services, communities that were essentially off-limits to the local population. Workers from the south came for one or two years, worked long hours, were given free flights back to the south at regular intervals, left when they had achieved their financial goals, and had virtually no contact with the North apart from flying over it to and from their work camps.

Many communities had grown haphazardly, and governments realized that they had to be rebuilt based on proper surveying and planning for schools, hospitals, sewage, water, and other facilities. One major example was Aklavik in the Mackenzie Delta. It was subject to flooding so the government built the new town of Inuvik, some 55 kilometres away. Many people chose to remain in the old town. At the radar bases, Inuit villages were deliberately located some distance away, and the Inuit were forbidden access to some base facilities.

Other changes were revolutionizing the lives of the original people, including access to phones, electricity from diesel generators, radio, and TV. When they went back on the land, skidoos had replaced dog sleds. In the new communities, serious gulfs developed between those who welcomed the new lifestyle and those who pined for the old ways, and between old and young. When new jobs failed to replace the loss of work and income from hunting and trapping, idleness led to loss of self-respect, pride, and self-confidence, and increasing problems with alcohol and violence. While governments sought to help, those efforts sometimes exacerbated problems. Civil servants were sent from Ottawa while local graduates remained unemployed.

By the late 1950s, the federal and territorial bureaucracies had grown to over 3,000, one civil servant for every three or four families. In spite of this growth, federal policy remained largely ad hoc and uncoordinated. First Nations were administered by the Department of Indian Affairs, which seemed at times more dedicated to paternalism and self-preservation than to First Nations rights or concerns. The Inuit, however, had the same rights as other Canadians, and were administered by all the federal departments with interests in the North. Since 1867, the goal of Indian Affairs had been assimilation; other departments did not always share that goal. In the 1950s, the pendulum seemed to swing in favour of maintaining some separate identity for First Nations but for integrating the Inuit more closely. One result of these changes was that, in just one generation, the Inuit went from being almost completely ignored by the federal government to being intensely studied, administered and showered with government programs and attention.

For the majority of Northerners, the fur trade was still the most important sector of the economy when the Second World War ended. Unfortunately, the demand for furs as well as the price were extremely poor for decades, and by 1965 the fur trade accounted for less than 5% of the economy. That was catastrophic for Aboriginal peoples. It made welfare payments a very significant proportion of their income, and hastened their movement into communities with the subsequent loss of their culture. Governments tried to arrest the decline in wildlife through tighter regulations for hunting and trapping, but such regulations were applied to Aboriginal peoples who depended on game for food. Charging poor Aboriginal hunters fees for licences was symbolic of thoughtlessness. Southerners also successfully pressed government to enforce conservation laws that met their values and interests such as a ban on the selling of wild game meat, a ban which further weakened the traditional way of life.

To provide alternative employment, Ottawa encouraged the production of handicrafts—carvings made from soapstone, bone and ivory, and prints, clothing, and knick-knacks. By 1960, a huge proportion of the population—over 2,000 people—were engaged in the handicraft industry. The government began providing training and financial assistance for Aboriginal businesses. There were few opportunities or markets, so these efforts often failed. The federal government also encouraged the development of co-ops to market furs, fish, and handicrafts, to provide retail stores, and to manage housing projects. The co-ops were quite successful, partly because they conformed to the traditional culture of community activity. They also had a very significant side-effect as some of the managers emerged as political leaders, and the co-ops became a nursery for political activism. In 1963, representatives from 18 co-ops from all over the Arctic met at Frobisher Bay. It was the first such meeting of Aboriginal leaders in history, an important step in their growing assertiveness.

The government continued to put its faith in mining as the engine of growth for the northern economy, but the results were disappointing. Mining was inherently unstable because of huge swings in global demand and prices. High transportation and other costs made it particularly marginal in the North, and many mines opened and closed with the cycles. Governments often offered support such as buying gold when world demand declined. While extensive exploration revealed many mineral deposits, most were too small or remote to attract investment. New mines were opened or re-opened: the Eldorado silver and radium mine at Port Radium, the Mayo-Keno mines in the Yukon, a lead and zinc mine at Pine Point on Great Slave Lake, a copper mine at Yellowknife, nickel-copper at Rankin Inlet, and a mine on Baffin Island. In the same period, oil and gas production declined at Norman Wells, and Yukon Consolidated Gold Corporation closed down in 1966 after more than six decades.

Many of the federal policy thrusts received a major boost when John Diefenbaker led the Conservatives to victory in the federal election of 1957. The Conservative regime was the first in Canadian history that was not dominated by voters, bureaucrats and interests from the Quebec City-Windsor corridor. Diefenbaker believed firmly that the regions outside Central Canada had been ignored and exploited by Toronto and Montreal. He set out to create balance in federalism with new policies aimed at strengthening Atlantic Canada, the prairies, and the North. The Conservatives believed that Canada had become too close to the United States, and too influenced by "Made in America" policies in defence, economics, culture and other areas. Diefenbaker believed strongly that all Canadians were equal and should have the same rights, privileges, and advantages. That meant giving First Nations the vote in 1960, raising their standards to something comparable to that of the general population, increasing the influence and participation of Northerners in their own government, and transferring responsibilities and personnel from Ottawa to the North.

These attitudes crystallized in the 1958 federal election in which the main government policy was the "Northern Vision." It was billed as a second National Policy, the first one being the development of Canada from east to west, the new one being development from south to north. It was the first time northern issues figured prominently in a Canadian election. It caught the imagination of many southern Canadians, and helped produce the biggest electoral landslide up to that time. The government set about putting meat on the bones of its rather vague desire to have Canadians look north rather than south, to see the North as a distinct part of their identity and therefore different from the American identity, and to develop the resources of the North for the benefit of all Canadians including, this time, those in the North.

One of the ablest ministers—Alvin Hamilton—was put in charge of a re-organized department of Northern Affairs and Natural Resources, whose size and budget were substantially increased. This new department included Indian Affairs, though the goals of economic development and protecting local populations sometimes clashed. The government's approach was comprehensive, and included a huge increase in funding for research which promoted the development of academic studies of the North. By 1963, the federal government had almost 4,000 employees working on or in the North. It was the biggest employer in the territories, and federal spending constituted over half the region's gross domestic product.

The centrepiece of the Northern Vision was the Roads to Resources program, which pumped billions of dollars into building roads and railroads to tap the resources of the North as well as the northern regions of the provinces. The Mackenzie Highway was pushed farther north to Wrigley. A major link was the all-weather Dempster Highway which connected Dawson City to Fort McPherson and Inuvik. When it was completed in 1978, it was the first road to reach Canada's Arctic shore. Roads were pushed into the Yukon mining towns of Keno and Mayo. The railroad was extended to Great Slave Lake making it possible to develop the large deposits of lead and zinc at Pine Point. River and air transportation facilities were also expanded, and communications networks steadily improved as more communities obtained access to phone services, radio, and TV.

During this period Ottawa also sought to stimulate the resources side of Roads to Resources with a wide variety of incentives. Mining companies obtained tax write-offs for investments and reduced fees for exploration. The government built hydro-electric plants to provide electricity to mines and large communities such as Yellowknife, and supplied diesel generators to other communities. These incentives helped produce a wave of exploration, which stimulated the economy. Some new mines were opened, but the program did not fulfill the dreams of its proponents either because not enough new mineral deposits were found or because they still proved too costly to develop. After 1963, the new Liberal government carried on with most of the programs, but never again would a "Northern Vision" dominate federal politics and occupy such a large place in the national psyche.

New roads were not exclusively about mineral resources. Until the 1950s, governments made little effort to encourage tourism, fearing its negative effects on Aboriginal people. The plight of Dawson City helped change that. It had never recovered from the end of the gold rush. Gold mines continued to operate, but they were marginal. The city was finally connected to the outside world by road in 1955, but that was a mixed blessing as it put the Yukon River sternwheelers out of business. It made little sense to leave the capital in Dawson, and in 1953, it was transferred to Whitehorse.

Practically the only thing Dawson had left was its heritage, now reduced to little more than Robert Service's log cabin and some run-down buildings and boats. Canadians then rediscovered its exciting and unique past when Pierre Berton published *The Klondike* in 1957. The federal government decided to make it a major tourist attraction, something now possible because of the highway link. One of the gambling casinos—the Palace Grand—was restored, along with the sternwheeler *Keno* and a number of buildings. A theatre was built and named after Diamond Tooth Gertie, one of the more colourful creatures from the days of the gold rush. In 1964, Ottawa promoted a major celebration called The Dawson Gold Rush Festival, and the number of tourists doubled. Other attractions in the Yukon—the historic district of Whitehorse, Miles Canyon, the Chilkoot Trail, panning for gold, and the wildlife and scenery—were exploited as the federal and territorial governments pumped money into hotels, motels, restaurants, and parks. In 1972, Ottawa established Kluane National Park, home to Canada's highest mountains.

Throughout this period territorial government evolved very slowly towards the immediate goal of more local involvement and influence and the very distant goal of provincial status. In 1945, Whitehorse had the only elected municipal government in the North, and the Yukon had the only MP. This constituency was expanded to include the Mackenzie River Valley, which became a separate constituency in 1952 and was extended to the whole NWT in 1958. In 1979, the NWT was divided into two constituencies, giving the North a total of three MPs and a substantial over-representation in terms of population. Ottawa still firmly controlled territorial government, but local involvement and influence was gradually increased. Federal civil servants were replaced on the territorial councils, sometimes by people from the North. In 1946, a Northerner was appointed Commissioner. In 1952, the NWT Council began holding two meetings a year, one of them in the NWT, and a year later it obtained the right to borrow money subject to Ottawa's approval.

In 1951, residents of the NWT were allowed to elect three of the eight members of the Council. Four were elected in 1954, then five in 1963 giving elected members a majority. In 1960, the government began selecting its appointed members of the council from outside the civil service. By 1964, only two members of the Council were civil servants, though they held the two most powerful positions: Commissioner and Assistant Commissioner. In the Yukon, Whitehorse gained elected municipal government, something Dawson had enjoyed between 1901 and 1903. Although Ottawa remained firmly in control, these steps were important in ensuring that fewer and fewer decisions were made with complete disregard to the views and knowledge of Northerners. The next two decades would see continuations of the trends begun after the Second World War.

Chapter 9

Self-Rule

Diefenbaker's Northern Vision and his government's Roads to Resources program were not particularly successful during his period in office. In the late 1960s, however, the efforts did lead to the opening of a number of mines—asbestos at Clinton Creek in the Yukon, lead and zinc at Keno and Faro in the Yukon and at Ross River in the NWT, copper at Yellowknife, and tungsten and silver in the NWT. Gold mining experienced a resurgence in the Yukon when the price rose sharply in the 1970s, and diamonds became important in the NWT in the 1990s. There were, however, major disappointments: the closure of the Faro mine in 1984 was a disaster for the Yukon economy, the Keno mine was unstable economically, the Yellowknife copper mine closed in 1981, and the Pine Point lead-zinc mine closed in 1987. Mining, nevertheless, provided a steady stimulus to the economy in terms of exploration and improvements in transportation such as ice roads and other infrastructure.

The Liberal government of Lester Pearson that replaced Diefenbaker was even more aggressive in its determination to develop the North's oil and gas reserves and to Canadianize the energy sector. It issued more exploration licences, subsidized exploration, and supported Canadian-owned companies such as Dome Petroleum. In 1975, the government of Prime Minister Pierre Trudeau created a government-owned company, Petro-Canada, which was given a privileged position. In spite of favours to Canadian companies, it was Imperial Oil that made a major find off Tuktoyaktuk in the Mackenzie Delta in 1970. That re-opened the question of building a pipeline to carry oil and gas to the networks that spread from Alberta to the rest of North America.

First Nations immediately expressed concerns with the effects such a pipeline would have on their lives and the environment. The federal government responded in classical fashion, by appointing a Royal Commission to undertake a study. Often such commissions were used either to prepare public opinion for an initiative the government has already decided to launch or to shelve some issue for future debate. This Commission was different because the government selected Thomas Berger to head it, and his natural sympathies lay with the local population and environmental issues rather than with government or big business.

Berger selected a competent staff and made a specific point of taking the team and accompanying reporters to 35 Aboriginal communities to listen to ordinary people rather than having spokespersons come to the Commission to present their views. Every day the reporters and the CBC carried the comments of local people into the living rooms of southern Canada. What Canadians heard shocked them. One after another, people expressed grave reservations about how a pipeline could damage their lives. They told stories of how they lived, bringing that insight for the first time to a huge TV and radio audience across Canada. They talked of how such a project would interfere with the migrations and breeding of wildlife, especially caribou, and how fish would be poisoned. They knew what they were talking about because only three decades earlier the Alaska Highway and the Canol Pipeline had been built without consulting them, without regard for their concerns, with little benefit to them, and with considerable damage to the environment, to wildlife, and to their health and welfare. On the other hand the companies could not satisfactorily answer questions about how they would construct a pipeline over permafrost and deal with other potential problems so graphically identified.

Berger's report—*Northern Frontier, Northern Homeland*—was published in 1977, and was so well written and illustrated that it became a best-seller. The implications of the report came as a shock to southern Canadians because it really said that the interests of the inhabitants of the Mackenzie River Valley came first, and the North was no longer just a frontier territory to be exploited by the rest of Canada. The enquiry led to a huge improvement in Canadians' understanding of their own North and its inhabitants. Berger recommended that the pipeline project be shelved for ten years, and that it not be built at all until land claims were settled. The latter recommendation put pressure on Ottawa to deal with the claims, and meant that the recommended 10-year moratorium was a minimum period rather than a definite start-up date.

Berger's report and the publicity it received were so powerful that the government had no option but to accept it. The companies themselves decided to shelve plans to exploit Arctic energy because of the magnitude of the problems identified in exporting that energy to southern Canada, the enormous costs, a decline in the international price of energy, the discovery of large reserves in northern Alberta and British Columbia, and federal policies they regarded as unfair. Even though exploiting Arctic oil and gas was uneconomic, the federal government continued to push development. The National Energy Policy of 1980 provided for massive federal involvement in the sector, a favoured position for the government-owned Petro-Canada, and discrimination against private and foreign-owned companies. Exploration remained an important part of the economy, but development did not occur. Indeed, the Mackenzie Valley Pipeline was not approved by the National Energy Board until 2010, at which time the plans of private companies were still on hold. One legacy is that everyone knows that enormous reserves exist, a pipeline can be built, and that energy will be available when it is needed.

The Berger Report gave a major thrust to the settlement of land claims in the Mackenzie River Valley. Pressure to settle them across the North had been mounting for years, and claims dominated much of the political discourse over the next several decades. Because there was almost no agricultural land, the federal government knew that only a tiny fraction of the North would be occupied by non-Aboriginal people in isolated communities or used as roads. Aboriginal people were free to roam over 99% of the landscape as they always had, without any interference by the government, and hopefully without needing any support. In Ottawa's view, the territories were all "Crown Land," and would remain undisturbed except for the small areas granted or sold to outsiders or set aside for mines, roads, and communities.

This ambiguous policy did not deal with the question of what rights Aboriginal peoples actually enjoyed and what happened when their hunting, fishing, and trapping rights were encroached upon. The Crown might "own" all the land in theory, but what of the land Aboriginal people actually lived on and used? During the Yukon gold rush such issues could be ignored because the influx of 30,000 outsiders vastly outnumbered the local population, the development was limited to a very small area, and very few Aboriginal people were affected by it. The construction of the Alaska Highway was very different. In southern Canada a road or railroad did not adversely affect farms next to the road allowance. In the Yukon, the Highway affected the local people because the workers killed wildlife, polluted rivers and spread diseases. As the pace of economic activity increased throughout the North after the Second World War, hunting, fishing, and trapping were harmed over huge areas adjacent to the still-small areas occupied by newcomers from the south.

Ottawa could no longer avoid dealing with the land claims, and circumstances had changed in the Aboriginal peoples' favour. The rapid change in lifestyles had created new problems and exacerbated old ones, making people more determined and impatient for solutions. In spite of their manifest problems, the schools had produced a population that was basically literate. More and more students were emerging from universities, versed in law, politics, and history, with skills such as negotiating, public speaking, and public relations. Territorial governments were now more powerful, more democratic, and more representative of local peoples. Their grievances were well known, including the fact that the federal government kept repeating mistakes such as announcing major developments without consultation. In southern Canada there had been a sea-change in attitudes, with a new-found interest in human rights, minority rights, equality, justice, and environmental concerns replacing paternalism, a cultural superiority complex, and a belief in uncontrolled exploitation of resources. Churches, for example, had completely reversed some attitudes and were now promoting the preservation of local culture. There was also a growing awareness of problems in the North such as alcohol abuse and of the fact that southerners had contributed to the problems through misguided policies and sexual abuse. TV and radio were now making these local issues national, and the courts were increasingly sympathetic to them.

In Ottawa, however, old habits died slowly. In 1969, Jean Chretien, Minister of Indian Affairs in the Trudeau Liberal Government, issued a White Paper on Indian Affairs. Reflecting the philosophy that all Canadians should be equal, it proposed that First Nations reserves be abolished and their populations fully integrated into Canadian society. The Department of Indian Affairs was to be abolished, with many of its responsibilities transferred to the provinces. Ignoring many lessons from history, the civil servants and politicians who drafted the document did not consult the people affected by it. First Nations did not see it as progress towards equality with other Canadians, but rather as an attempt to destroy the rights they had retained or obtained in centuries of negotiations. It was rejected out of hand, and Ottawa quietly shelved the proposals. It was also noted that Ottawa wanted these changes to come into effect before it settled land claims. The damage had been done, and the infamous White Paper was one of the misguided federal gestures that helped galvanize a new militancy across the North.

The first claim to be settled was that of the 2,500 Inuvialuit, the Inuit of the Mackenzie River-Beaufort Sea region. They had created an organization called the Committee for Original People's Entitlement or COPE. Their claims were relatively limited compared to those of some other groups. They wanted to be compensated for any rights they surrendered, to be consulted about any developments that occurred in their region, to preserve their culture, and to have clear ownership of some of the land. Ottawa did not find these demands unreasonable, and the claim was settled in 1984, with the Inuvialuit giving up the right to exclusive use of the region in return for full rights on 13,000 square kilometres, more limited rights on 95,000 square kilometres, a share in royalties on resource revenue in the entire region, a cash payment of $150 million over 13 years, additional funding for development, specified hunting and fishing rights, and a guarantee that they would be involved in future economic developments. The Inuvialuit Regional Corporation was established to manage the funds and quickly became a dominant player in the economy.

A settlement in the Yukon proved to be far more difficult. There were sharp disagreements and serious misunderstandings between Aboriginal peoples and other residents. The latter dominated the Yukon government, but the negotiations which began in 1973 were between Ottawa and the Aboriginal peoples even though the discussions were the most important political, economic and cultural event in the territory. The concerns of the non-Aboriginals were lessened when they realized that Aboriginal leaders did not want to seize control of everything, that Ottawa was willing to spend millions in the territory as part of an agreement, and that Ottawa accepted that the government of the Yukon government had to be involved. An agreement was worked out after three years of difficult negotiations, but was rejected when put to a vote. In all such negotiations Ottawa insisted that the agreement extinguish all rights not specifically covered so that no future disputes over land ownership could arise to hold up economic developments. Aboriginal peoples refused to accept this clause, and the talks failed. Agreement was finally reached in 1992 for an umbrella arrangement that provided individual bands with $250 million and recognition of outright ownership of 44,000 square kilometres of land. By 2005, 10 of the 14 bands had settled their claims under this agreement.

The most militant group was the Dene of the Mackenzie Valley. Their rights were theoretically covered by Treaties #8 and #11, which Ottawa had imposed in 1899 and 1921 when it felt it was necessary to extinguish rights to clear the way for economic development. When those developments failed to materialize, Ottawa lost interest in implementing the terms of the treaties. Promised reserves were never demarcated, and in time people questioned whether it made sense to grant 640 acres of land to each family when the families were nomadic hunters. At the Berger hearings a number of seniors also said that they had been tricked and coerced into signing the treaties, calling their very legitimacy into question.

Anger had been growing amongst the Dene for decades if not generations, and it exploded during the Berger hearings. In 1975, they issued the "Dene Declaration," which stated that the Canadian and NWT governments were not their governments, that they were a separate nation, and that they wanted, in effect, a separate state within Canada. They demanded full control within that territory, including control of banking and some relations with foreign governments. It was too extreme a document to be a useful basis for negotiations, and talks with Ottawa failed. As a consequence the Métis and several bands of Dene broke away and negotiated separate settlements with Ottawa in the early 1990s.

The last of the four major negotiations involved the 15,000 Inuit of the central, eastern, and northern Arctic. The demand was led by the highly effective Tapirisat organization. These negotiations were complicated by the fact that in the eastern Arctic the Inuit majority wanted a territory separate from the NWT which was dominated by the Mackenzie Valley region. It was decided to proceed with the land claims and then deal with the question of political division. Once that decision was made, the land claims in the eastern Arctic were easy to settle. The settlement in 1993 gave the Inuit a cash grant of $1.2 billion to be paid over 14 years plus outright control of 350,000 square kilometres of land, making their corporation the largest landholder in North America.

With the land claim out of the way, the eastern Inuit concentrated on the goal of separating from the NWT. One factor in their favour was that the creation of a separate territory dominated by an Inuit government would strengthen Canada's sovereignty claims since the Inuit had lived there for thousands of years. The eastern and northern Arctic was quite distinct from the Mackenzie Valley geographically, ethnically, and economically, and it made little sense to administer it from Yellowknife. The main question was the border, with Métis living several hundred kilometres east of the Mackenzie River preferring to remain in the NWT. They lost that battle, and the western border of Nunavut followed the tree line northwest from the border with Saskatchewan, giving Nunavut over two million square kilometres of territory, 20% of the entire land surface of Canada. Nunavut, meaning "our land," was created on April 1, 1999, with Iqaluit, formerly Frobisher Bay, as its capital.

Nunavut was unique in that the Inuit constituted 80% of the population. They copied the NWT system of government by consensus rather than adopting the British system of political parties, government and opposition, as the Yukon had done. That had the advantage of making it more difficult for narrow interest groups to influence decisions. The first election—on 15 February 1999—produced an Assembly of 19, including 15 Inuit. One of them—Paul Okalik—was elected Premier by the Assembly. The official languages of the territory were Inuktituk, English, and French.

The land claims negotiations took place during a period of devolution of federal power to governments in the North and of increasing democratization of those governments. In 1965, political control of the North still remained a virtual monopoly of civil servants and politicians in Ottawa, and much of the developing bitterness in the North stemmed from the continuous imposition of decisions in which local people had little input and which were often unsuitable and sometimes completely unrealistic. In the 1960s and 70s, the devolution and democratization that began after the Second World War accelerated dramatically.

For the Yukon, Ottawa established an executive council or cabinet in 1969 containing the Commissioner, several officials and two Members of the Legislative Assembly or MLAs. By 1977, elected MLAs were in a majority, and some of them were of Aboriginal origin. Conservatives introduced party politics and won 11/16 seats in the 1978 election. Their leader—Chris Pearson—became Premier and appointed a cabinet of Conservative MLAs. Finally, the Yukon had Responsible Government. The position of Commissioner became largely ceremonial, but federal programs and funding remained extremely important so Ottawa continued to be a major player in Yukon politics. In 1985, the New Democratic Party formed a government under Premier Tony Penikott, indicating that the two-party system was entrenched and working properly. That government paid more attention to Aboriginal concerns and remote areas, but the Aboriginal MLAs did not function as a bloc. Throughout this period, jobs and many responsibilities were transferred from Ottawa to Whitehorse, with government becoming the major employer in the Territory. While provincial status received a great deal of attention in the 1970s, there was little progress towards obtaining it, and it ceased to be a major political issue.

In the NWT the local administration was moved to Yellowknife in 1967 from Fort Smith where it had been located since 1921. In 1965, the first Aboriginal was appointed to the Assembly, and two years later the first one was elected. By 1970, the executive consisted of 4 appointed Councillors and 10 MLAs and the NWT had Responsible Government. Five years later, all 15 Assemblymen were elected, 9 of them being Aboriginal. The Assembly was expanded to 22 in 1979 with Aboriginal candidates winning 14 of the seats. Unlike the Yukon, the NWT did not adopt the party system, and policy making and the selection of the Premier and Cabinet were by consensus, a system that conformed to local tradition. As in the Yukon there was a steady flow of jobs and responsibilities from Ottawa, but the federal government remained a very powerful presence. Government was also the largest employer in the Territory.

Canadian sovereignty over the mainland and islands had not been disputed since the 1920s, but claims to sovereignty over Arctic waters was a different matter. In 1969, the Americans sent the tanker *Manhattan* through the Northwest Passage to determine if Alaskan oil could be delivered to the Atlantic. Canadian icebreakers had to be used, and the oil companies concluded that the route was too dangerous. Canada extended its territorial limit from 3 to 12 miles, which made some but not all of the channels Canadian, and sought support for control of a 100-mile pollution zone. The United States did not accept these steps, and sent the Coast Guard icebreaker *Polar Sea* through the Northwest Passage in 1985 without requesting permission from Ottawa. Canadians were outraged, and Washington agreed two years later that in future it would request permission though it still insisted that the waters were international. Countries bordering the Arctic have since agreed that problems such as sovereignty will be settled peacefully, but they have not yet agreed on whether the waters are Canadian or international. Asserting and protecting Canadian sovereignty in the North remains a major priority for government and the public, provoking high level visits, proposals for building huge icebreakers and various types of infrastructure, military expeditions, and ongoing diplomatic negotiations.

From the first "discovery" by Europeans in the sixteenth century, the Canadian North experienced a long, eventful, and complicated evolution leading to the current organization into three territories which might, someday, become provinces like their southern neighbours. Unlike in the rest of Canada, Aboriginal peoples constituted a very large proportion of the population, and hunting, fishing, and trapping remained important aspects of culture, society and even the economy. The spectacular Gold Rush left the Yukon with separate territorial status and a legend that eventually made tourism one of the pillars of its economy along with mining and government. But at 30,000, its population is smaller than it was at the height of the Gold Rush.

It was perhaps inevitable that the rest of the NWT would someday be separated from the region of the Mackenzie River Valley. In 1999, Nunavut became a separate territory, unique in Canada in that the Inuit constitute 80% of its population of 30,000. The NWT, which once stretched from the 49th parallel to Ellesmere Island and from Alberta to Labrador, now holds 45,000 people in the Mackenzie River Valley north of the 60th parallel. Within these territories the Aboriginal peoples gradually changed from nomads living on the land to an almost exclusively urban people concentrated in less than 100 communities. Over a century of effort to assimilate them was only partly successful, and aspects of their culture survived, revived, and now flourish. While the territories have not achieved provincial status, it is now clearly understood that the Canadian North belongs to the people who live there. Its future and its place in the Canadian mosaic will reflect the views, interests, and decisions made by the Inuit, the First Nations, the Métis, and the other relative newcomers who permanently inhabit the Land of the Midnight Sun.

Suggestions for Further Reading

Given its small population, the Canadian North has been well served by historians. Decades ago Morris Zaslow wrote exhaustive accounts of the North, which included the Canadian Shield. Since then, two outstanding historians, William Morrison and Kenneth Coates, have written extensively on specific topics and, what is so important to our overall understanding of a region, summarized their own work and that of others in several excellent books. The Dictionary of Canadian Biography and Wikipedia provide quick and easy access to much detail, and this text benefited from excellent comments from a number of expert readers. The following are the main secondary sources for this book.

Bone, Robert M. *The Geography of the Canadian North.* Don Mills, 2003

Coates, Kenneth. *Canada's Colonies. A History of the Yukon and Northwest Territories.* Toronto, 1985

Coates, Kenneth and William Morrison, eds. *For Purposes of Dominion. Essays in honour of Morris Zaslow.* Toronto, 1989.

Coates, Kenneth and William Morrison. *Land of the Midnight Sun, A History of the Yukon*, Edmonton

Dickason, Olive Patricia with David T. McNab. *First Nations.* 4th ed. Don Mills, 2009

Grant, Shelagh. *Polar Imperative.* Vancouver, 2010

Morrison, William. *True North, the Yukon and Northwest Territories.* Toronto, 1998

Newman, Peter C. *Empire of the Bay.* Toronto, 1989

Warkentin, John. *A Regional Geography of Canada.* Scarborough, 2000

Zaslow, Morris. *The Opening of the Canadian North, 1870-1914.* Toronto, 1971

—*The Northward Expansion of Canada, 1914-1967*, Toronto, 1988

—*The Northwest Territories*, 1905-1980. Ottawa, 1984

Index